# A Muse in Disguise

# A Muse in Disguise

## HOW HEARTBREAK INSPIRES CREATIVITY

*Dori Gilinski*

ISBN: 0615859445
ISBN 13: 9780615859446
Library of Congress Control Number: 2013914147
Aleph Publishing, New York, NY

# Contents

# Introduction

———

HEARTBREAK MAY TAKE MANY FORMS, but anyone with a heart knows what it is—or at least, how it *feels*. Heartbreak hurts, both physically and mentally. You can feel the ache in your chest. You can hardly think of anything except the overwhelming pain and what caused it. Everywhere you turn, there is a reminder of what has happened to you. You are completely consumed. You wonder how, or *if*, you will survive.

There are many ways in which your broken heart can heal all by itself, but what if you don't think you can wait? Moreover, what do you do *while* you wait? How can you be consoled when heartbreak is inconsolable? You pick up a book of poetry. You gaze endlessly at a reproduction of your favorite painting. You read a novel, watch a movie, listen to music....

The ways you can wallow or be uplifted seem endless. But you want to do something more than immerse yourself in the pain or simply feel better. You want to *understand*. You want to be *whole* again. To do these things, you need to learn how to cope, and not in a pop psychological way that merely offers superficial mantras. You need something more robust, something *meaningful*.

Hence, I offer this *philosophical* guide to heartbreak. When your heart breaks, there is a process through which you heal. Here you will be introduced to the three stages in this process, or three approaches to heartbreak: 1. Suffering 2. Retreating 3. Accepting and overcoming.

First, you feel the pain and you suffer. This is of course a painful step, but it is an important one in your development as it propels you to be creative. As you will see, this is the seed of creativity being planted through suffering. As you are immersed in suffering, which is by nature a negative and undesirable emotion, your first instinct will be to retreat from your reality—to escape in order to avoid the pain of suffering. As you will see in Chapter Two, the flower of creativity is again blooming: As you retreat from suffering, you not only escape your hostile reality; you also engage with ideas outside of yourself, which will serve as distractions and will water the plant that will later grow into a flower of creativity. Finally, the process of growth comes to an end when you are able to overcome your heartbreak by accepting it. You neither wallow and *feel* pain as you did in Chapter 1, nor do you try to escape your feelings. In Chapter Three, you learn to confront your heartbreak by accepting the reality of what you are going through and finding the strength to overcome it. You learn to live despite pain, despite suffering, despite heartbreak. In fact, you are liberated of your heartbreak and learn to create meaning and happiness for yourself. The process of growth culminates in finding our own meaning—not in trying to find meaning in the suffering itself, but in weaving heartbreak into something beautiful for YOURSELF.

Each approach is analyzed through specific artists and thinkers. Chapter One, introduces us to two modes of suffering by way of Pablo Neruda's and Pedro Salinas's poetic images of heartbreak. These twentieth-century poets can, in turn, be situated within the context of the fourteenth-century Italian poet, Petrarch. In this chapter we learn that some heartbreak is self-inflicted. By idealizing the beloved, these poets make authentic engagement with another human being impossible. Love is not reciprocated, and heartbreak ensues. The creativity generated by the unique sort of suffering that is endured because it is of their own making allows the poets to repeat the cycle: feeling the pain of heartbreak, healing, and, as a result, being creative.

Chapter Two explores retreat as a response to suffering. Through a study of artist Salvador Dalí and poet Frederico García Lorca—both twentieth-century Spaniards—we see how the artists use retreat as a response to heartbreak, in both their personal and interpersonal relations.

Chapter Three analyzes the influence of the nineteenth-century German philosopher, Friedrich Nietzsche, on the twentieth-century Greek artist, Giorgio de Chirico. Both were deeply influenced by the Ariadne myth. Examining these relations gives us insight into the concept of acceptance and overcoming as a response to heartbreak. Wholly and unconditionally embracing this suffering enables us to affirm our life as our own—and all that comes with it.

It is worth considering that these approaches may, for some at least, be stages en route to wholeness: One experiences loss and the longing that accompanies it. One suffers and perhaps retreats as a response. Eventually, one comes to embrace, or at least to accept, the suffering, and this is leveraged to overcome the heartbreak. There is no single prescription for treating heartbreak. As universal as heartbreak is, it is also singular. Each of us is introduced to it in our own unique way. Nevertheless, it is my view that the three chapters in this book speak to the most profound types of heartbreak and responses to it.

Each of these concepts—suffering, retreating, and overcoming—needs to be understood. We need a *theory* of suffering, for example. Each of the artists and thinkers will provide us with ways to think about these concepts: They will provide us, directly or indirectly, with significant theories, and these will serve as our "guide to heartbreak."

Ultimately, the three approaches have a common ground in the concept of creativity. Suffering and loss—what we call "heartbreak"—inspires creativity. In this guide, through a study of the biographies and works of famous poets, philosophers, and artists, I hope to show just what creativity is, and how it can be an avenue for overcoming a broken heart.

I welcome you on this journey. We have all taken it and many will do so again. But now, with this guide, we are not without ways to make sense of what we have endured and perhaps to make it meaningful.

# CHAPTER 1

# THE BENEFITS OF SUFFERING

JUST WHAT IS IT TO love another human being and not be loved in return? What is it to yearn for another who is absent? To long for them even while they are in your arms?

Or is this something else altogether, not love, but perhaps obsession? *You* are yearning. *You* are longing. *You* are gazing. Yes, love seems to be *something*—a feeling, a state of being, or even a psychological condition, but where is the beloved? Where is the other consciousness? What is love without the confrontation, the slow dance of tentative engagement, the clashing of swords, the passionate embrace of another?

Yet this is one version of love, as cultivated by poets who idealize their beloved, elevating her until she is unattainable. And there, in the far-off distance of perfection, she becomes everything the poet can ever want but will never have. She is the horizon he will never meet. And though she breaks his heart because of this, she also makes his art possible. It is *he*, in fact, who creates his own heartbreak, the fertile ground for the poetry that begins the cycle once again. After all, *she* is not allowed to participate as she truly is. *He* has created the conditions for love—that is, for the love he wants. She is a mere reflection for him; here there is no authentic interaction between two people who are groping and grappling with each other. She mirrors his own desires and thoughts. Whatever she is in herself remains a mystery. Consequently, the relationship is between the lover and his own thoughts, his own desires, his own projections. It is a version of narcissism that often presents itself as victimization at the hands of unrequited love, but that also, just as often and perhaps ironically, presents itself as an opportunity for exact the sort of suffering that is required to create beautiful works of art!

A certain sort of poet depends on the impossibility of the relationship for his poetic output and, by positioning himself as a tortured creator, can write verses that are the products of the trials and tribulations of his suffering. Suffering becomes an aphrodisiac that not only heightens the lover's desire but thereby also enables him to write. In this tradition, love cannot be a reciprocal relationship in which both partners play an equal role; rather, gender roles must be clearly established to prevent the male from quenching his "eternal thirst." The dilemma that emerges from desire and the impossibility of its fulfilment causes the lover's pain, which impels him to write. Could it be that for this sort of poet, as George Santayana insisted, the development of the soul can arise only through an initiation of pain, and thus that poetry can arise only through pain?: "The soul, too, has her virginity, and must bleed a little before bearing fruit."[1] At least for the three poets that are the focus of this chapter, exquisite poems are the "fruit" born of love affairs—real or imagined.

While emotional suffering is something that most people try to avoid, these poets show us that it can forge a valuable pathway for introspection, personal transformation, and the creation of deeply moving poetry. Their love poetry is inspired by the complex relationships they had with real-life women, relationships that changed the poets and how they viewed and experienced life.

To ensure that their burning desires could never be quenched, the poets assigned traditional gender roles to the lover and the beloved, placing the latter on a pedestal that would forever be beyond the lover's reach. The relationships that emerge in Neruda's *Veinte poemas de amor y una canción desesperada* (1924, first translated into English as a collection titled *Twenty Love Poems and a Song of Despair* in 1969[2]) and Salinas's *La voz a ti debida* (1933, translated into English as *My Voice Because of You* in 1977[3]) illustrate the poets' unequal footing with the superhuman beloved. Salinas explicitly constrains the female's ability to desire the lover by distancing her from him. She appears otherworldly: "Tú no puedes quererme: estás alta, ¡qué arriba!" ("You cannot love me: you are loftily high!"). The closer the beloved's proximity to the heavens, the more pathetic the human lover becomes, even to himself. By positioning himself to have his heart broken, the lover invites the pain and suffering that consume him and compel him to write poetry.

For Neruda and Salinas, the benefits of suffering in solitude outweigh the benefits of finding happiness with a real-life woman. Like Petrarch before them, both poets reject the contentment they might experience if their beloveds were to return their love. They fear that fulfilment of their desires will inevitably stifle their creativity, so they choose a misery that helps them connect with and express the human experience of unrequited love.

## THE IDEAL OF LOVE

What's interesting about the triad of fourteenth-century Italian humanist Francesco Petrarch and the two twentieth-century poets who were influenced by him, Chilean poet Pablo Neruda and Spanish poet Pedro Salinas, is that the conception of love embraced by Petrarch influenced young poets hundreds of years later—young poets whose lives were very different from Petrarch's as well as from each other's. Petrarch abandoned a future in law to train and work as a cleric, which left him time to pursue his main passions, Latin literature and writing. Neruda, born not only hundreds of years later than Petrarch but also continents and oceans away, was less interested in academic matters than in political ones. A devoted communist, Neruda became a poet–diplomat for the Chilean government and traveled widely as part of his duties. Salinas was an academic and literary critic. Though there are clearly differences between these men in terms of their vocations and their contexts, as well as their ages—Neruda was just a teenager when he wrote his poetry, while Salinas was an adult university professor—features of their poetic worldviews are remarkably similar. And given the success of Neruda's early work (no other Spanish-language book of poetry has been more commercially successful), it's clear that countless others appreciate this worldview as well. But why?

Love poetry from the Renaissance through the Romantic era is known for its idealization of women, and Petrarch is one of the poets from the Renaissance era who is well-known for placing his beloved far above himself. The story goes that he fell in love with a woman, Laura de Noves, whom he saw in the church of Sainte-Claire d'Avignon. Whether she actually existed is unknown, but in any case, at least the *idea* of her inspired his best-known poetry. As Lord Byron mused in a discussion of Petrarch's *Il Canzoniere* (*The Song Book*), "Think you, if Laura had been Petrarch's wife/He would have written sonnets all his life?"[4]

While twentieth-century poetry is not defined by the characteristics of traditional romantic love poetry, some poets continued to follow in Petrarch's footsteps. Pablo Neruda and Pedro Salina composed poems depicting their beloveds not as the women they actually were, but as the women the poets wanted them to be. It is an open question whether longing is fundamentally selfish, regardless of the context, but we can safely say that the only longing this sort of poetry expresses is that of the poet, the lover, in relation to *his* own satisfaction. The woman, the beloved, continues to be a sort of prop for the poet, an object onto which he projects his desires.

This was no secret, for example, to Salinas's real-life lover, Katherine Reding, the woman who inspired the poem "La voz a ti debida." On the back of an envelope containing a love letter from Salinas, she wrote, "Beautiful letter in which he assures me that he loves me *as I am*—which, poor dear, he could never quite do except when my actions coincided with his ideas."[5] This is a perfect description of a consciousness unwilling or unable to truly and fully engage with another consciousness *as it is*. And this is, perhaps, because it is impossible to do so within the framework these poets have created. After all, if the beloved is *ideal*, she will not be manifest in this world. She may be the conception of perfection, a mind-dependent entity like a sort of caged bird in the poet's mind, or she may be a Platonic Form, eternally and immutably existing in another realm. In either case, she will never— she *can't* ever—be enfolded in his embrace. As Petrarch so feverishly declares:

> (6)
> Sí travïato è 'l folle mi' desio
> a seguitar costei che 'n fuga è volta,
> et de' lacci d'Amor leggiera et sciolta
> vola dinanzi al lento correr mio,
> (My mad desire has gone so far astray
> Pursuing her, who turned away to flee,
> And, free and clear of all the snares of Love,
> Runs easily ahead of my slow pace,)

(20)

Vergognando talor ch'ancor si taccia,
donna, per me vostra bellezza in rima,
ricorro al tempo ch'i' vi vidi prima,
tal che null'altra fia mai che mi piaccia.
(Sometimes, ashamed that I have not been rhyming
To praise your beauty, oh, my gentle Lady,
I let my mind go back to your first sight;
No other beauty moved me after that,)
(21)

Mille fiate, o dolce mia guerrera,
per aver co' begli occhi vostri pace
v'aggio proferto il cor; mâ voi non piace
mirar sí basso colla mente alter
(I've offered up my heart, but you don't deign
to glance down from your elevated mind;
if any other lady wants my heart
she lives in weak and much-mistaken hopes).[6]

Like Petrarch, both Neruda and Salinas use real women as
their points of departure. Salinas had Katherine Reding,
while Neruda had many lovers. They appropriate qualities
and traits of these women and then fill in the blanks with
their imaginations to elevate imperfect mortals to ideal beloveds. As such, these women serve as empty canvases on
which the poets can paint as they wish. The poets take on the
active role of "lovers" and begin remodeling the real women in

their lives by assigning them the passive role of the "beloved," who is then placed on a pedestal, just out of the poet's reach. This makes equality unobtainable and sets the stage for unrequited love, which appears to inspire these poets more than the women themselves. We can see, for example, that there is a wide chasm between the beloveds depicted in Salinas's *La voz a ti debida* and Neruda's *Veinte poemas de amor y una canción desesperada* and the real-life women.

Neruda's own name is perhaps autobiographical evidence of his desire to be seen in the tradition of Dante—he wanted to be a tragic poet. Neftali Ricardo Reyes Basoalto was anxious to conceal his identity when he first began publishing poems in local papers and journals. His father was a strict man who probably would not have approved of his son's frivolous activities; he expected Ricardo to forge a successful professional career. However, the reason for the pseudonym is less relevant for our purposes than the name itself. Oxford Spanish Literature Proffessor and Neruda scholar, Dominic Moran has suggested that Neruda may have taken it from Dante's star-crossed lovers, Paolo and Francesca, since he enjoyed casting himself in the role of the tragic Paolo, and he signed several of his pieces using the Italian version of the name rather than the Spanish.[7]

It is significant that the references to real women are ambiguous in Petrarch's *Il Canzoniere* (*The Song Book*), Neruda's *Veinte poemas de amor y una canción desesperada,* and Salinas's *La voz a ti debida,* which led the poets' critics—and even some of their friends—to doubt that their poetry was inspired by real women. For example, Petrarch's friend and patron Giacomo Colonna, bishop of Lombez, accused Petrarch of entirely inventing the beloved in *Il Canzoniere*. Petrarch refuted the accusations. In a letter, he declaimed: "You say that I invented the beautiful name of Laura ... so that others would speak of my (poetic) merit, ... that indeed there was no Laura except the one in my poetic imagination.... I wish indeed that she had been a fiction and not a madness."[8]

But Petrarch's letter didn't convince the bishop, because the depiction of Laura in the poetry is so glowingly positive and his desperation so intense that it's difficult to believe he's writing about a mere mortal. The same could be said about Petrarch himself—about each of these poets, for that matter. The man becomes the heartbroken lover and tortured poet. In so doing, Petrarch himself becomes a sort of mythical character.

However, what interesting claims the critics make! What Petrarch's dissenters imply is that no real person could inspire the sort of beautiful language and intense devotion that is found in the poet's work. Perhaps. Perhaps it is impossible for "real" love to reach the heights and intensities of idealized love. But are the feelings any less real because of this? And what of the tortured lover and poet himself? Is the conscious creation of this self a mere myth? That is, without the actual woman with whom the poet engages, we might ask: What is the reality of the poet who creates her?

Neruda and Salinas both attempted to escape similar questions about the existence of real-life inspirations for their poetry. The seemingly endless inquiries beg the question: Why were readers so determined to find out whether the poems are based on real women? What is it about the way these poets portrayed their beloveds that led readers to find fault with the portrayals and question the existence of real women behind them? These women, be they either real and then remoulded or entirely imagined, are mythical. In this rarefied air, love itself becomes purer and clearer—we can grasp it in a way that's not possible when there is an admixture with the temporal, finite, physical realm. Here's where the poet can find both love and himself without the contaminating features of another self. We can return to the Platonic notion of the Forms, the perfect, originating entities for everything that is.

In his *Symposium*, Plato explains this ideal in the context of love as a *search* for one's other self. It's only when he connects with his "other" that a man can become whole. Our modern-day description of our partner as our "other" half or "better" half is an echo of this view. Perhaps, then, Salinas's collection might be a meditation on love and human nature rather than an exploration of a specific relationship the poet was having or had already had. The fact that the original title of *La voz a ti debida* was *Poemas de una mujer y de un hombre* (*Poems of a Woman and Man*) suggests that Salinas was writing about a generic man and woman who experience universal love and loss.[9] The same suggestion can be made about Neruda's *Veinte poemas de amor y una canción*. But we mustn't overlook the fact that Neruda's poems are written from the perspective of a realist who sees love as a natural force. The pagan, sexual undertones in this collection are certainly *not* idealistic. Does this mean that our basic thesis about retreat from engagement with another consciousness is wrong? Consider these lines from Poem 14:

> Quiero hacer contigo
> lo que la primavera hace con los cerezos.
> (I want to do with you
> what spring does with cherry trees.)

Spring is a season of primal beginnings, newness, fertility. It is anything but ethereal. Mention of spring, then, provides a context for seeing Neruda's work as a *physical* yearning, reflected as an earthly quality in the *Veinte poemas*. Neruda's poetry is always tangibly sensuous. The intimation is opaque, to be sure, but certainly not subtle enough to transcend the earthly plane. His desires are in the real world, not the purely intellectual one. There must be some woman, some specific body, who drives him on. Nevertheless, Neruda's beloved will always break his heart. Influenced by Schopenhauer's concept of the will as an endless wanting, yearning, striving, and desiring, Neruda's longing occurs here and now, in this world, but it is never satisfied. The world, Schopenhauer argues, is not a rational place; rather, it is a place where a non-rational will underlies all our urges.

But regardless of whether we see Neruda, Salinas, and Petrarch as realists or idealists, they were motivated by something more than their beloved. For example, Salinas's work often seems more concerned with his philosophy of human nature than with the beloved, even though his emotions and real-life experiences with Katherine were what drove him to pour his heart out onto the page. And where Salinas's yearning is metaphysical, Neruda locates his urgent, unquenchable longing in the physical world. His poetry is always tangibly sensuous; his desires play out in this world. Indeed, he tells us about an early fumbling sexual encounter with an older woman on a threshing floor in his hometown of Temuco. His later sexual exploits in Santiago earned him the appellation "Don Juan." It's as if he's unwilling to sever his subjectivity, his *will*, and become pure mind or cognition, which is free from desire. He *wallows* in the flesh, in the earth, in feeling.

And there were perhaps other motivations for declining to dedicate love poems to identifiable women. In fairness to the critics, the poets seem to have been purposely vague about their muses. When Salinas's biographers tried to pin him down on whether his poetry was inspired by a real woman, he said:

> Seres reales, figuras, figuraciones? Los biografistas quieren descubrirlas, a lo policía, con todas sus señas … cuando lo cierto es que lo más definitivo y característico de estas criaturas … proviene de su creador; de la imaginación inventora del poeta.
> (Real people, shapes, configurations? The biographers want to discover them, to police, with all their

signs ... when the truth is that the most definitive characteristic of these creatures ... comes from their creator; of inventive imagination of the poet.) [10]

Spoken like a true poet, but not the truth. While Salinas may have fooled critics, love letters and a memoir stored in an archive at Harvard University Library reveal that, as we mentioned earlier, his muse was his real-life lover, Katherine Reding.[11] Reding's memoir *La amada de Pedro Salinas* (*The Beloved of Pedro Salinas*) and 355 letters exchanged by the couple were discovered in 1999 when the archive was opened at Smith College. In the memoir, Katherine writes:

> Los críticos ... tenían motivo s para dudar de la existencia de una *amada* viva. Los versos les parecían un trabajo de la imaginación, *un amor cerebral.*
> (The critics had reasons to doubt the existence of a living, breathing beloved. To them, the verses seem a work of the imagination, a cerebral love.) [12]

While Katherine's presence was veiled in *La voz a ti debida*, it's clear that she was unveiled in his bed. We might be tempted to judge Salinas for his complicity, but he did this with good reason. While he was infatuated with Katherine, Salinas was married to Margarita Bonmarti and had two children. His illicit affair followed in the tradition of Petrarch and courtly love before him.[13] Petrarch's Laura was married, so Petrarch's love for her was never consummated. Rather than experiencing her as a flesh-and-blood woman, Petrarch could forever hold her in his mind as pure, chaste, and even quasi-divine:

> (11)
> Lassare il velo o per sole o per ombra,
> donna, non vi vid'io
> poi che in me conosceste il gran desio
> ch'ogni altra voglia d'entr'al cor mi sgombra
> (I've never seen you put aside your veil,
> for sun or shadow, Lady,
> not since you learned about the great desire
> that drives all other feelings from my heart).

Considering their circumstances, we can understand why Petrarch and Salinas chose not to acknowledge their real-life lovers, but Neruda was a well-known playboy. So why the secrecy? Jorge Edwards, a Chilean novelist and journalist, quotes Neruda as confiding that "*no era una sola, eran muchas*"[14] (there wasn't just one lover, there were many). Neruda later wrote in his memoirs:

> Siempre me han preguntado cuál es la mujer de los *Veinte poemas*, pregunta difícil de contestar. Las dos o tres que se entrelazan en esta melancólica y ardiente poesía corresponden, digamos, a Marisol y a Marisombra.
> (I am always being asked who the woman in *Veinte poemas* is, a difficult question to answer. The two

women who weave in and out of these melancholy
and passionate poems correspond, let's say, to Marisol
and Marisombra.)[15]

By giving his lovers nicknames instead of naming them out-
right, Neruda was able to create more distance between his
reality and his poetry and minimize the role that his real
lovers played in his poetry. "Marisol" and "Marisombra":
Maria-sun and Maria-shadow. Maria, Mary. Mother Mary.
Mary Magdalene. Virgin. Whore. No woman, no *real* woman can simply be *a woman. This* woman.

To compound matters, speculation continues regarding
who these Marias may have been. Two principal muses have
been identified as Teresa Vásquez León ("Marisol"), his childhood sweetheart from Temuco, and Albertina Rosa Azócar
("Marisombra"), a fellow student at the Instituto Pedagógico
de Santiago. Marisol was called "Teresa Leon Battiens" (and
known as Teresa Vazquez). Neruda affectionately referred
to her as "Terusa." Marisombra was Albertina Rosa Azócar,
the sister of poet Ruben Azócar, Neruda's close friend.
Neruda met her at the Pedagogical Institute in 1921—there
are 104 surviving letters that he wrote to her that confirm
that Albertina Azócar was Neruda's first big love, and he
remained in love with her long after the publication of the
*Veinte poemas* while he was on consular duty in the Far East.
Even when Neruda returned to Chile in 1932, he continued
to pursue her as a married man. Neruda himself coyly provides few biographical facts about either woman. Instead, the
women become poetic objects in his hands. Marisol is the

love from the enchanted provinces with immense night stars and has eyes dark as the rain-soaked sky of Temuco. She appears with all her joyfulness and lively beauty on almost every page, surrounded by the waters of the port and the half moon above the mountains. Marisombra is the student from the capital, with a grey beret and the gentlest eyes, embodying the ever-present honeysuckle fragrance of fleeting student love and the physical release of passionate encounters in the city's hideaways.

Since Neruda took the truth about which woman inspired which poems to his grave, the precise role that flesh-and-blood women play in *Veinte poemas de amor y una canción desesperada* will never be known. Naturally, this leads to more conjecture. Perhaps, it has been suggested, it's impossible to separate them, since they are often fused into one.[16] What may seem like inconsistencies may actually be the projection of the poet's desires that were elicited by more than one muse.

This may explain how Neruda's beloved could be both "morena" ("dark") *and* "palida" ("pale"). Poem 19, in which the woman is described as "morena y ágil" ("brown and agile") with a "cuerpo alegre" ("happy body"), was written for María Parodi, who we can assume shared some of these qualities.[17] In Poem 3, when Neruda describes a woman with a "cintura de niebla" ("waist of fog"), we see the influence of Albertina Rosa Azócar. But ultimately, a poet isn't limited by the constraints of reality, so his beloved can have qualities that appear to be contradictory if that's what his imagination conjures.

This is obvious in Salinas's *La voz a ti debida*, where his beloved is constantly changing on the page, but real life was a different story. In her foreword to Salinas' Houghton Library archives, Katherine Whitmore (originally Reding) writes, "Mi querido Pedro, con su amor y nostalgia inventó verdaderamente su infinito" ("My dear Pedro, with his love and nostalgia, truly invented his own infinity"). [18]

This is interesting in itself, but we can understand Salinas's tendency even better when we know that perpetual change is also a traditional Petrarchan conceit. By bestowing a volatile nature on his beloved, Salinas could express and clarify his thoughts on the nature of reality, which, as I noted earlier, is one of his poetic preoccupations. By using gender stereotypes and "female" character traits that are easily recognizable, Salinas conveys the changeability of the beloved. At times, we see her as a perfect being, bathed in images of clarity and light, but elsewhere she becomes fickle and vain.

The changing nature of the beloved in this collection provides a hint that Salinas is writing about a real woman, because it reflects the classic "infatuation turns to resentment" cycle that characterizes so many relationships. If his beloved were merely an imaginary muse of his own making, what reason would he have to become disenchanted? *La voz a ti debida* is a poetic manifestation that conveys the natural course a romance takes: The lover falls in love and idealizes the Other, as seen in the earlier poems, and when the relationship goes sour, he begins to resent her, as seen in the later poems.

So I conclude that Salinas, Neruda, and Petrarch were all *influenced* by real women. And while their creativity ultimately took over to fashion beloveds who were larger than life, in each case flesh-and-blood women were the basis or starting points for the poets' inspiration. But by *idealizing* the women as they do, the poets detach themselves from entanglements. From this vantage point, they may indeed be able to reflect on love in its purest state, but in doing so, they preclude not only the possibility that they will themselves ever bask in its glow but also the possibility of actual love with a real person and all the vicissitudes that come with it.

Although Petrarch used the figures of the yearning lover and the unattainable beloved, he didn't invent the genre. The figures and the theme of unrequited love can be found in the poems of French troubadours from the twelfth century, two centuries before Petrarch was born. But the similarities end there. For one thing, the troubadours' descriptions of women tended to be very precise, whereas Petrarch could be vague about his beloved's physical appearance, as he demonstrated in *Il Canzoniere*. Perhaps this was because Petrarch was more enchanted by his idealized version of his beloved than by the flesh-and-blood woman herself. What does this say about his conception of love? What is there about the human condition—or is it a male condition?—that makes one want to *remake* another for himself? One possible explanation of this behavior is that we have one consciousness attempting to make his world. As a starting point, this is not unreasonable. You have no other experience of consciousness but your own. You go out into the world—remember your smallest self, you as a child, and how everything was new—and you touch this, taste that, sniff and see and hear. You are absorbing and assimilating the world. And then one day you meet *another* consciousness. You are *confronted* by it. Perhaps you both reach for the same flower at the same moment. That is when you realize that the world is also *for another.* What is the next step? What does it take to interact with another consciousness? What will be the result?

But what if, instead, you withdraw? In that case, you have saved yourself the trouble of engaging with the other, but you will also experience loss and be left to wonder, "What if?" What if you had stepped forward into the confrontation? Thus for Petrarch, for example, the image of his beloved represents the merging of his own desires with the sorrow and pain of an unrequited love. And this also seems to be true for Neruda in *Veinte poemas de amor y una canción desesperada* and Salinas in *La voz a ti debida.* Like Petrarch, both of these twentieth-century poets recreated their real lovers as their poetic beloveds, leaving the women's full realities unwritten, and so not only preserving their perfection but also avoiding the vicissitudes of human interaction.

Why didn't these poets simply create their beloveds from the wellsprings of their imaginations? Why use actual, and therefore flawed, women as their templates? One answer would be that understanding that these poems were inspired by the poets' real-life yearnings and amorous disappointments gives readers a window into their worlds and, in the process, joins poet and reader together in love and heartbreak.

# THE POETIC REALITY

Salinas and Neruda both had living muses, but the poets don't merely recount their experiences, and they also don't unthinkingly embrace Petrarchan images. Instead, they re-fashion the ideal Petrarchan beloved to convey their own versions of her. Neruda uses the Petrarchan model to express his ideas about sensuality and eroticism, and Salinas conveys his thoughts on the nature of being. But like Petrarch, these two poets share the desire to transform reality into what Salinas called "una fabulosa operación de la fantasía que es incomparablemente más que la simple dúplica, copia o repetición" ("a fabulous product of fantasy that is incomparably more than the mere duplicate, copy or repetition").[19]

Of poetry itself, Salinas had this to say:

El oficio del poema no es reproducir aquella primera experiencia, sino crear otra, la obra, nueva, distinta, libre en su nuevo ser, en modo alguno esclava de su punto originario. El mundo de las formas artísticas es vida, claro. Pero no es la vida ésta, el trabajo multitudinario de ir y venir, de dormir y despertarse, de amar y desamar por el mundo. Es otra vida.

(The office of the poem is not playing that first experience, but creating another, new, distinct, free in its new being, rather than being a slave to its original point. The world of art forms is life, right. But not this life, the massive job of coming and going, sleeping and waking, to love and fall out of love. It's another life.)[20]

Here we can explicitly see the idea of a consciousness endeavoring to *create* his world out of the elements at hand. It is in this "other life" that Salinas anchors *La voz a ti debida*. His beloved, who fits the description of the traditional Petrarchan female with *her* "tierno cuerpo rosado" ("rosy body"), is also contemporary: on her wrist she wears a "reló" ("wristwatch"; Poem 1), she drapes her body in a "traje verde" ("green dress"; Poem 8), and she walks in "tacones altos" ("high heels"; Poem 50).[21] Through these descriptions, Salinas makes it clear to us that his beloved is not the timeless woman carved in marble. Whether his muse, Reding, really wore a green dress or had a penchant for high heels is less important than what these images represent in the poetic beloved, namely the materialism Salinas rejects in favor of trying to reach and connect with the beloved's *metaphysical* essence. The imagined beloved becomes a manifestation of Salinas's desire for substance, reality, and essence, similar to the Platonic ideal previously described.[22] The poems in which the beloved is fickle and vain aren't just poetic artifices but are rather expressions of the differences between poetic lover and poetic beloved. Salinas must first dress his beloved in frocks so he can *de*frock her and reduce her to her true nature. In Poem 14, the poetic voice says to the beloved:

Quítate ya los trajes,
las señas, los retratos;
yo no te quiero así,
disfrazada de otra,
hija siempre de algo.

Te quiero pura, libre,
irreductible: tú.
(Take off your clothing,
Features, pictures;
I don't want you like that,
Masked as another,
Always daughter of something.
I want you pure, free,
Irreducible: you.)

Salinas adorns his beloved with female characteristics throughout the collection so that he can strip them away to reveal what Salinas describes in this poem as "the irreducible you."[23] A curious tension that has been lurking all the while now comes to the fore. There is the yearning for the essence of the Other, but at the same time, the Other is eliminated—that which is no longer *this* pair of eyes and *those* lips is an *idea*. Is that what love is, an escape from what there is to what could never be? We hope to find a lover who is perfect, who doesn't have the qualities we despise in ourselves: laziness, weakness, dishonesty, stupidity, corruptibility, and so forth. We want our lover to be stripped of all our personal faults. So we want our lover to be inhuman in order to project ourselves onto her. Perhaps this is more obsession with unrealizable perfection than it is actual love. But if this is true, we are once again left with the question, "What is love?" For someone like Salinas, however, perhaps this question leads to ruminations on existence. Salinas's poetry is fundamentally underlined by existential preoccupations and inquiries into human nature.

However, whereas Salinas's poetic depiction of the beloved in *La voz a ti debida* has a cerebral, reflective tone, Neruda's beloved is blooming with sexuality—but is no less idealized for it. In the first poem in Neruda's collection, we encounter a beloved who is described in overtly erotic language. Julio Cortázar said Neruda "nos arrancaba a la vaga teoría de las amadas y las musas europeas para echarnos en los brazos a una mujer inmediata y tangible […] con las simples palabras del día" ("pulled us out of a vague theory about loved ones and European muses to throw us into the arms of an immediate and tangible woman … with the simple words of daily life").[24]

But it's important to note that European muses are not entirely missing from *Veinte poemas de amor y una canción desesperada*. In many respects, Neruda's beloved does embody the Petrarchan woman, but Neruda, a man of the twentieth century, does not rely on the delay of sexual gratification for motivation, as Petrarch had five hundred years earlier. Unlike Petrarch's *Il Canzoniere*, a collection in which he struggles with the conflict between Christianity and the sinful nature of the erotic, Neruda's work depicts lovers in the midst of a sexual act, with no concern for religious doctrine. Fundamentally, what Neruda wants from the beloved is the consummation of his desire.[25]

Neruda's fixation on the physical manifestation of love is apparent from the outset. The first poem in this collection plunges us into sexuality and immediately focuses our attention on the naked female body and its parts: "cuerpo de mujer, blancas colinas, muslos blancos" ("body of woman, white hills, white thighs"). It's easy to imagine her lying much like Titian's *Venus of Urbino*—pale, docile, waiting for her male counterpart to initiate sex. The woman is introduced to us in her carnality and presented as a composite of isolated body parts that, together and separately, have a powerful sexual connotation: "muslos" ("thighs"), "piel" ("skin"), "pecho" ("breasts"), "ojos" ("eyes"), "pubis" ("pubis"). It is left to the reader to put her together.

Here again we might interpret Neruda in terms of one version of the idealized woman: body parts and not a whole being, woman waiting for man and not a person in her own right, with her own ideas, personality, foibles, hopes, fears, and sexuality. And with her thus dismembered, she is silent. In her silence, she is whatever the poet says she is—but the poet, in turn, is forever separated from her. Neruda also uses this strategy in Poem 15: "Me gustas cuando callas" ("I like it when you're silent"), and Salinas uses it in his poem: "Lo que eres me distrae de lo que dices" ("What you are distracts me from what you say"). This is one of the most famous poems in the Spanish language, often recited by heart by romantics. What does the fact that the beloved is only a fiction projected and gazed at through the male lens say about us? That she is silent, she is infantilized, and, worse yet, adored for it? That in the end, the poet takes a peculiar pleasure in the thought of her dying?

While the undisguised eroticism in this poem may seem lewd and perhaps even dehumanizing, Neruda is using techniques that follow an established tradition linked to Petrarch. The fetishized listing of a woman's body parts—hand, arms, eyes, mouth, forehead—can be found in Petrarch's Sonnet 200:

> Non pur quell'una bella ignuda mano…ma l'altra, e
> le duo braccia…li occhi sereni e le stellanti ciglia, la
> bella bocca angelica…e la fronte e le chiome
> (Beautiful naked hand ... but the other, and the two
> arms ... eyes serene and starry eyelashes, the beautiful
> angelic mouth ... and her forehead and hair).[26]

The first poem in Neruda's collection, "Cuerpo de Mujer" ("Body of a Woman"), introduces us to a pale figure. Her flesh is made white to stress that she's distant and idealized. The white body of Neruda's beloved appears again in Poem 3, where we're presented with a "cintura de niebla" ("waist of mist") and "brazos de piedra transparente" ("arms of transparent stone"). Neruda's descriptions bring to mind a still, lifeless statue, not a woman consumed by animalistic passion and desire. Inert, she is simply awaiting him to bring her to life—which is a paradox given that it's her ideal perfection to which the poet runs as a means of escaping himself.

Beyond mentioning it, I haven't said much yet about this idea. As we began thinking about each poet's vision of love, I focused on the question of the idealized woman, be she extrapolated from an existing individual or created whole cloth from the poet's imagination. But what of the poet himself? What sort of man *makes* woman? Part of the answer to this question is as old as any creation story. We've all heard the account in Genesis. Still another way to answer this question elaborates on a suggestion I made earlier—that consciousness seeks to make the world for itself. This idea is also not new.

The question of whether the world is discovered or created has troubled philosophers for millennia. One of the most well-known answers comes from the German philosopher Georg Wilhelm Friedrich Hegel (1770–1831). Human consciousness moves through stages or shapes. Starting with sensory perception, consciousness takes all immediate sensory data as certain. But the singularities soon give way to *concepts*—consciousness is capable of more than the flux of particulars. At this point, consciousness has no concept of self. After all, everything has apparently just *been*—this grape, that sound, those trees. Consciousness of things is not the same as being *aware that one is conscious of those things*. To think of oneself as a subject for whom some things are known is a rather different order of consciousness from the one we began with. *Self*-consciousness, Hegel maintains, requires intersubjectivity; it requires *another* consciousness. According to Hegel, this confrontation is dramatic—and traumatic— with each of the two consciousnesses prepared to fight to the death for recognition.

If we take this idea of the development of consciousness by way of confrontation and engagement with another consciousness, we can see that it's not possible to grasp love when it's idealized beyond the poet's reach. Ironically, the poet who wants to make the world for himself *is trying* to make meaning. He may also believe that he is trying to *uncover* meaning but is perhaps deluding himself about this. If he can create a woman who is utterly lovely and ideal but who also says yes to him, miserable wretch that he is, then he's valuable. Yet he created the very being who is then saying he's worth something!

## The Contrasted Lovers

It is not only the creation of an impossible beloved that sets these poets up for heartbreak and suffering. Grief is built into their self-images. These men are miserable wretches whom only the perfect beloved can save. But since there is no chance for love to be reciprocated, the poets are doomed to endless despair.

Both Neruda and Salinas describe the beloved as a sort of unattainable goddess they believe will bring the lover out of his loneliness and misery. The poets begin by describing the male as imperfect, incomplete, and unworthy of the beloved's affections. We also see this tendency in Petrarch. For example, in Sonnet 306 of *Il Canzoniere*, Petrarch describes the beloved as the sun that showed him the "glorious steps" to heaven. In her absence, he's reduced to a lonely, wandering animal:

Ond'io son fatto un animal silvestro,
che co pie' vaghi, solitarii et lassi

porto 'l cor grave et gli occhi humidi et bassi
al mondo, ch'è per me un deserto alpestro.
(And so I have become like some wild beast,
bearing on lonely weary wandering feet
through this unfriendly world a heavy heart
and eyes that are continually downcast).[27]

Both Neruda and Salinas reuse and further develop the Petrarchan image of the wanderer in a hostile landscape. In the first poem in *Veinte poemas de amor y una canción desesperada*, the lover describes himself as "solo como un túnel" ("alone like a tunnel") before meeting his beloved:

Fui solo como un túnel. De mí huían los pájaros
y en mí entraba la noche su invasión poderosa.
Para sobrevivirme te forjé como un arma,
como una flecha en mi arco, como una piedra en mi
honda.
(I was alone like a tunnel. The birds fled from me,
and night entered me with its powerful invasion.
To survive myself I forged you like a weapon,
like an arrow in my bow, like a stone in my sling.)

Neruda establishes the lover as a tortured and solitary figure who hopes the beloved will relieve him of his pain before he's inevitably thrust back into it. The first line of the stanza is abrupt and fragmented by the period. Splitting the thought into two distinct sentences results in a stunted flow, creating a sense that the poet is struggling to convey a dark and painful memory. The simile of the lover who is as dark as a tunnel is especially poignant because it is contrasted with the expansive and flowing description of the beloved's alabaster body in the previous stanza, which is heavy on imagery: "Cuerpo de mujer, blancas colinas, muslos blancos, / te pareces al mundo en tu actitud de entrega" ("Body of woman, white hills, white thighs, you look like the world in your attitude of giving"). It's also relevant that a tunnel is empty, while the beloved is literally full of life.

The stanza describes past events, painfully etched into the poet's memory, with a meekness that suggests he was helpless and couldn't surmount the sadness and darkness around him. The gloomy night, more powerful than he, violently tormented his existence. The poet was fighting a losing battle against its "invasión" ("invasion") until the beloved became the "arma" ("weapon") against his misery. The early poems in the collection reflect Neruda's happiness and bliss, but as we move further into the collection, his sadness reemerges and he finds himself alone again. The last word in the "La Canción Desesperada" ("The Song of Despair")—"abandonado" ("abandoned")—confirms this.

In *Veinte poemas de amor y una canción desesperada* and *La voz a ti debida,* the lovers and their beloveds are rarely presented as actual couples. The relationships are described through a clear distinction between the "yo" ("I") and the "tú" ("you"). This reinforces the distance between them and also the disparity between the lover, who is fallible and weak, and the beloved, who is sometimes rendered as almost divine. The "yo" and the "tú" are at different levels, almost inhabiting different planes of reality. To describe them as "nosotros" ("us") automatically places them on the same plane, and the poets often need the distance that the different planes provide for them. Neruda describes the lovers as "nosotro"s only once in the whole collection, when it's all over: "Nosotros, los de entonces, ya no somos los mismos" ("We, of that time, are no longer the same"). Lover and beloved aren't conjoined in blissful harmony, because the beloved is always just beyond reach—a situation that's a hallmark of the Petrarchan tradition.[28]

In the first line of La *voz a ti debida*—"Tú vives siempre en tus actos" ("You live always in your actions")—Salinas speaks of the beloved female as a creator of life: "Con la punta de tus dedos / pulsas el mundo" ("With the tip of your fingers you palm the world"). The poet desires a beloved who's defined by her vitality, one who holds and plays the world with the tips of her fingers the same way that mere mortals might play a violin or a piano ("es tu música"). The glorification reaches its peak in the final verse of the stanza: "La vida es lo que tú tocas" ("Life is what you touch").

Neruda describes the beloved with similar language in Poem 14. In the opening line, "Juegas todos los días con la luz del universo" ("Every day you play with the light of the universe)", the description of the female as whimsically "playing" with the light stands in sharp contrast with the somber description of the lover throughout the collection. In the seventh stanza, Neruda writes: "Couanto te Habra dolido acostumbrarte a mi, a mi alma sola y salvaje, a mi nombre que todos aheyentan" ("How you must have suffered getting accustomed to me, my savage, solitary soul, my name that sends them all running"). He describes himself as the antithesis of the beloved whom he sees as divine. As we know, there is no unmediated communion with the divine. And, yes, although any interaction is to some extent mediated through language, skin, thoughts—with a real person standing before you, someone whom you reckon with as an existing individual, there is at least a *chance* that you may be consoled. Meanwhile, if the beloved is equated with love itself, not only is the lover always alone, but so also is the beloved. Yet we mourn for the lover in a way we do not mourn the beloved—or at least we mourn for him first and maybe only later for her.[29]

Meanwhile, line two of the poem refers to the beloved as a "visitadora" ("visitor"), which suggests a sense of awe; she is certainly far from commonplace. She's like a spirit or angel who doesn't live in the world of the poet but merely pays it a brief visit. In Salinas's *La voz a ti debida*, the lover is constantly awed and surprised to be in the beloved's orbit. In Poem 1, he writes that the infallible beloved's only mistake was falling in love with him:

Y nunca te equivocaste,
más que una vez, una noche
que te encaprichó una sombra
- la única que te ha gustado-.

Una sombra parecía
Y la quisiste abrazar
Y era yo.
(And you were never wrong.
Only once. One night when
you fell in love with a shadow
(the only one you cared for).
It seemed a shadow.
And you wanted to hug it.
And it was me.)

Although this may sound extreme to the twenty-first-century ear, it's not unusual for the lover to describe himself as a mere shadow who's given life when he's "touched" by the beloved. Depictions like these can be found in the poetry of Petrarch, Ovid, Virgil, and Dante. It's not until the beloved embraces him that the lover has access to an exalted reality, one that can be reached only through the act of loving and being loved. The lover's existence is dependent on *loving*, as expressed by Spanish novelist and poet Miguel de Unamuno's character Augusto Pérez in the book *Niebla*, when he says: "Amo ergo sum" ("I love, therefore I am").[30]

Spanish literature scholar Carlos Feal Deibe writes that the beloved is "equiparada al amor" ("equated with love"):

Una sombra. El sí que está, de lleno, inserto en ese mundo moribundo, apenas existente. Mundo sin amor. Porque el amante, antes del encuentro con la amada, está solo, sin amor. ¿No está sola también? ¿Cómo, pues, no es una sombra, sino que por el contrario, se afirma tan tenazmente? Se introduce aquí una diferencia importante.

(A shadow. He is fully inserted in a crumbling world, barely existent. It is a world without love. Because the lover, before his encounter with his beloved, is alone, without love. Is she not also alone? How then is it that she is not a shadow but, on the contrary, so tenaciously self-affirming? An important difference is introduced here.)[31]

If the beloved were flesh and blood, she would also be solitary and made complete only by love. But by presenting her as divine, the poet casts her as self-sufficient and whole, in contrast with the lover's own incompleteness. The roots of this idea go back to Plato, who described the gods as being "whole" because of their absolute perfection. This is the real distinction between the lover, who is human, and the beloved, who is a goddess.

Salinas further explains the beloved's immunity to pain and sadness by equating her with love. For example, in Poem 62, the beloved and love itself are one and the same:

Cuando *tú* me elegiste
—*el amor* eligío—
salí del gran anónimo
de todos, de la nada.

(When you chose me—
love chose—
I came out of the great anonymity
from everyone, from nothing.)
The lover must stoically accept the pain he feels when
he longs for the beloved, knowing that he cannot rise
above his mortality and limitations.
Salinas laments this but resigns himself to his
situation:
Yo no puedo darte más.
No soy más que lo que soy.

¡Ay, cómo quisiera ser
arena, sol, en estío!
[…]
Pero
no soy más que lo que soy.
(I can't give you more.
I am no more than I am.

Oh how I would like to be
sand, sun, in summer!
[…]
But
I am no more than I am.)
Like Salinas, Neruda also elevates the beloved to the
level of a divine being, reducing himself to a flawed,
sorry mortal. Neruda writes in Poem 8,

Soy el desesperado,
la palabra sin ecos,
él que lo perdió todo,
y el que todo lo tuvo
(I am the one without hope,
the word without echoes,
he who lost everything
and he who had everything.)

He claims his words are so insignificant that they aren't even worthy of being repeated by an echo. He focuses primarily on his loss and uses the past tense—"tuvo" ("had")—to draw a contrast between his previous happiness with his beloved and his present state of misery. By referring to *himself* as "desesperado" rather than describing his *situation* as desperate—signified by the use of the verb "ser" rather than "estar," as used in "estoy desesperado"—he suggests that it's simply his nature to be desperate. The following couplet reiterates the hope he invested in the beloved:

Última amarra, cruje en ti mi ansiedad última.
En mi tierra desierta eres la última rosa.
(Last hawser (rope), in you creaks my last longing.
In my barren land you are the final rose.)

In accordance with the Petrarchan lyric, the second line compares the beloved to a rose,[32] yet as the word "última" ("last") suggests, the poet sees a bleak future for himself, now that his beloved—his last hope—is gone. His barren land is destined to remain barren.

His existence isn't wretched, however, simply because the relationship ended. The poet uses similar images in another poem, "He Ido Marcando" ("I Have Gone Marking"), to describe his life before the affair. This flashback shows the poet struggling, as he was in Poem 1, "Cuerpo de Mujer", to compose a complete sentence:

> La soledad cruzada de sueño y de silencio.
> Acorralado entre el mar y la tristeza.
> Callado, delirante, entre dos gondoleros inmóviles.
> (The solitude crossed with dream and with silence.
> Penned up between the sea and sadness.
> Soundless, delirious, between two motionless gondoliers.)

The image of a lonely lover awaiting his beloved in a deserted seaport is an often-used image that's immediately recognizable to the reader; Petrarch, too, makes reference to seaports in various sonnets. In "He Ido Marcando" the alliteration in the first line ("soledad, sueño, silencio") sweeps us up in the stanza's overwhelming sense of sorrow. The adjective "acorralado," generally used to describe a defenseless animal corralled in a pen, accentuates both the lover's feeble nature before the sea—the physical pen he finds himself in—and his sadness—the *emotional* cage he can't seem to escape, even if, like the one he purportedly built for his beloved, it is of his own making.

In the works of both Neruda and Salinas, the lover hopes to find strength in his beloved, not the weakness he recognizes in himself. This is why, at least in part, he assigns to her a perfection that he hopes will allow him to escape from himself. For Salinas, the escape fits within the Platonic tradition, in which love is seen as a form of ascent or becoming toward Being.[33] For Neruda, the escape is predominantly erotic; the fulfilment of desire allows the lover to briefly break free from what Schopenhauer describes as "the penal servitude of willing."[34] But Neruda's beloved can neither *permanently* elevate him to this higher state of being nor release him from the fundamental pain of living. Indeed, as one insightful critic observes, there is "always in Salinas the hand which reaches and never finds, the elusive and deceptive nature of reality, the *peau de chagrin* which shrivels up as its owner is on the verge of achieving his desire. And the search goes on, the eyes pierce deeper and deeper in their quest for the beloved."[35] So, what has this sort of love wrought?

## SUFFERING AND CREATIVITY

Petrarch, Neruda, and Salinas share a basic definition of love as a sort of longing or desire for something unattainable. Consequently, they see sadness and pain as the most lyrical aphrodisiac. Miguel de Unamuno, a Spanish poet, playwright and philosopher, similarly captures the notion of love as pain when he writes, "No hay verdadero amor sino en el dolor, y en este mundo hay que escoger o el amor, que es el dolor, o la dicha" ("There is no true love save in suffering, and in this world we have to choose either love, which is suffering, or happiness").[36] According to this definition, we simply cannot both love and be happy. The elation produced by love is fleeting, and the heights and depths of emotion ultimately break the lover's heart. But the suffering the lover endures is valuable. It is through accepting the inevitable aftermath of suffering that he can fully experience love and gain the insight and perspective he needs to live life completely. But do any of these lovers reach this goal?

In a word, no. Neruda and Salinas prefer to be dissatisfied poets rather than satisfied lovers. The poems in the collections discussed here lament the loss of a beloved, yet it is only through experiencing pain that the poet can become self-aware enough to be inspired and creative. It is only through the loss of the beloved that the poet gains objective distance from the relationship, which provides space for creativity. The poets embrace their solitude. Without having to confront another consciousness as a full, whole, complete being, they are able to continuously make and remake her, continuously make and remake their world, which will invariably collapse around them … and then they begin again.

Neruda wants to develop his solitude because it enables him to write poetry. If not for their suffering, the poets, the *lovers*, would have nothing to say.[37] This also shows up at the end of Salinas's *La voz a ti debida*, where his suffering leads him to an epiphany. The final poem of the collection is a rejection of the poet's established idealism, the position that separated the lover from the beloved. Ultimate reality, Salinas realizes, is material reality. Seventy poems into his collection, the poet turns away from his desire for an immaterial beloved and wishes she were "de carne y hueso" ("of flesh and bone"):

> ... ellas, desmelenadas, fieras,
> ellas, las sombras que los dos forjamos
> en este inmenso lecho de distancias?
> (those dishevelled terrible beasts,
> they, the shadows that we both forge
> in this great bed of distances?)

The image of a bed of distances suggests that sensuality and eroticism may bring the lovers together. The collection closes with an image of the beloved's "corporeidad mortal y rosa donde el amor inventa su infinito." ("mortal and pink body where love invents its infinity").

Similarly, Neruda's suffering reaches a climax in "La Canción Desesperada," where the memory of the beloved causes him to suffer:

> Oh carne, carne mía, mujer que amé y perdí,
> a ti en esta hora húmeda, evoco y hago canto.
> [...]
> Era la negra, negra soledad de las islas,
> y allí, mujer de amor, me acogieron tus brazos.

(Oh flesh, my own flesh, woman whom I loved and lost,
I summon you in the moist hour, I raise my song to you.
[...]
There was the black solitude of the islands,
and there, woman of love, your arms took me in.)

Like Orpheus, a legendary musician, poet, and prophet in ancient Greek religion and myth, Neruda triumphs over the pain through "evoco y hago canto" ("song and poetry"), and his amorous loss becomes a lyrical achievement: the poem itself.

The collection is rich with the poet's internal conflict: his unwillingness to fulfill "mi sed, mi ansia sin límite" ("my thirst, my boundless desire") for fear of losing his "dolor infinito" ("infinite pain"; Poem 1). When the beloved comes close to satisfying the lover's desire for her, the lover immediately pulls back: he prefers his "viejo dolor" ("old pain'"; Poem 5), which leads him to write beautiful verses, to the possibility of a happiness that would diminish his ability to write poetry. Between one poem (3) where the lover is enthralled by the desire to possess the beloved and admires her "voz misteriosa" ("mysterious voice") and another where he blames her for interrupting his solitude—"Eres tú la culpable de este juego sangriento" ("You are to blame for this bloody game," Poem (5))—the poet's attitude undergoes a dramatic shift. He begins by worshiping her as a divine being who is always beyond reach and shifts to perceiving her as a potential hindrance: "Todo lo llenas tú, todo lo llenas" ("You fill everything").

Amorous fulfilment *stifles* the poet's creative process, and he resents her for this because his misery feeds his creativity:

Antes que tú poblaron la soledad que ocupas,
y están acostumbradas más que tú a mi tristeza
(Before you, they (my words) peopled the solitude you occupy,
and they are more used to my sadness than you are).

Neruda *needs* to have the emptiness and solitude sink into his yearning and transform it into poetry. Bécquer, a nineteenth-century Spanish post-romanticist poet and tortured soul, used a fitting simile to describe a poet's attachment to his pain: "como guarda un avaro su tesoro, / guardaba mi dolor" ("like the miser guards his treasure, I guarded my pain"). [38]

In both *La voz a ti debida* and *Veinte poemas de amor y una canción desesperada*, the poets' suffering is responsible for identity crises that break their minds and hearts open to extensive self-analysis through writing poetry. The great divide between past and present also distinguishes between happiness and misery, emphasizing the poets' suffering.

Petrarch's prologue sonnet "Voi ch'ascoltate" ("You Who Hear") accentuates the growth he has experienced by rejecting his younger self as "altr'uom" ("another man"). The poem concludes with his realization that everything that gives pleasure is a dream: "che quanto piace al mondo é breve sogno" ("the world's delight is a brief dream").[39] Petrarch's suffering liberates him from the illusion of happiness as reality.

Salinas also treasures his pain, not only because it's the last remnant of his beloved, but also because it makes his life meaningful. Poem 63 reads:

No quiero que te vayas,
dolor, última forma
de amar. Me estoy sintiendo
vivir cuando me dueles.
(I don't want you to go,
pain, last form
of loving. I feel myself
living when you hurt me.)

To suffer—to feel pain—makes Salinas feel profoundly *alive*. As nineteenth century English poet Percy Bysshe Shelley notes in *A Defense of Poetry*, pleasure is a paradox: "The pain of the inferior is frequently connected with the pleasures of the superior portions of our being. Sorrow, terror, anguish, despair itself, are often the chosen expressions of an approximation to the highest good."[40] It is in the deepest depths of misery that the lover feels most intensely; that's where the poet becomes ennobled by his sorrow. He must preserve his pain and suffering to become "divine." Unamuno understood this when he wrote:

El hombre es tanto más hombre, esto es, tanto más divino cuanta más capacidad para el sufrimiento, o,

mejor dicho, para la congoja, tiene [...] Hay que pedirle
a Dios que se siente uno a sí mismo en su dolor.[41]

Man is all the more man, that is, all the more divine, the
greater his capacity for suffering, or better, for anguish. In
this world we are given the choice between love and happiness, and—poor fools!—we want both: the happiness of loving and the love of happiness. But we should ask for love rather
than happiness, for the latter allows us to doze off into habit,
and then we may fall asleep altogether, and without ever waking, lose consciousness forever. We should ask God to make
us conscious of ourselves in ourselves, in our suffering.)

Neruda and Salinas, like Petrarch, turn their backs on
love and the possibility of happiness so that they can strive
to become complete through their poetry. What began as a
seeming narcissism has, perhaps, transmogrified into tremendous self-sacrifice. For in a peculiar twist, these poets have
set themselves up for inexorable failure by refusing to engage
their beloved, by defining love in a way that is impossible
to achieve. And while we may feel dismayed that their beloveds are not allowed to be real, we may also mourn their
heartbreak.

CHAPTER 2

———

WHEN PEOPLE TALK ABOUT LOVE, they often talk about feeling "whole," as if they'd been searching for their other half until the very moment they fell in love. In fact, Plato gives us one explanation of why we feel this way. In his *Symposium*, a dialogue about love, Plato tells us a myth according to which, in primordial times, you and your "other half" were in fact a single being. Indeed, so the myth goes, human beings were hermaphrodites—creatures that have a single head with two faces on opposite sides. Hermaphrodites also had four arms and four legs—the better to hold on to themselves. These unified binary creatures were so powerful that an intimidated Zeus cut them in half. Ever since, each person has searched for their other half, in order to feel whole again.

This wholeness may be sparked by that electric connection you feel when you first meet someone and you find, through conversation, that your thoughts, likes, and dislikes seem so aligned that you think to yourself, "This person could only be for me." You find yourself feeling completely at ease, despite the fact that you have only just met this person. You might as well finish each other's sentences, or exclaim "I was about to say that!" as they tell you that their favourite writer is Goethe or that they hate ice cream. Everything fits. Everything is as it should be, because you are with this person and this person is with you.

It is in these minutiae, these small but significant details, that you find yourself falling in love. A new lover offers you a unique insight into another human being of a sort that you rarely have an opportunity to experience. For a period of time you escape your own experience, because you are able to experience life as a duo, in unison. After you bond over the symmetries between you and your lover, you eagerly learn to love the things your lover loves and to hate the things your lover hates, taking on many of your lover's preferences as your own. The difficulty with a breakup is that, by the time the relationship dissolves, you are no longer the same person you were at the start of the journey—you have become an amalgamation of the former you and the person you became with your lover. You have found a person who was not scared off by your strangeness, your phobias, your neuroses, and your modes of feeling and thinking—things you were sure would make you unlovable. You inevitably believe that your beloved is the only person on earth who will ever accept you without judgment and love you with complete knowledge of your flaws.

Your sense that you have known each other forever, that you belong together, and that you can't imagine not being with this person is so strong that when the relationship falls apart, when your other half leaves you, you find yourself once again feeling quite literally as if a part of you has been ripped away. You want to be whole again; you want to reconcile. If achieving wholeness once again seems impossible, you may want to escape, in order to flee this terrible evisceration.

"Heartbreak" is a strange word to use for what happens to you when your relationship ends. After all, nothing physical actually breaks inside you. Your internal organs remain intact. Perhaps it would be more apt to refer to it as a self-break, for what really happens to you is that a part of your self breaks away. The part of you that you had been missing before you met your beloved, that part of you that you had found, is now gone. And once again you are left feeling incomplete. This time, however, what you have lost is known to you. It has a name, a personality, and quirks and idiosyncrasies no one else had or has, for no one else is your beloved. Before the self-break, you were seeking, but your object was unclear. Now your loss is explicit.

This feeling of incompleteness—especially after you have experienced the euphoria of fusion with another, the warmth of human closeness and feeling understood—is a significant part of what makes heartbreak so difficult to get over. You are afraid, quite rightly, that you may never feel complete again. You have returned to being half a person, *you are lacking* in a profound way. It is, you believe, too much to bear. So, if you do not retreat from such devastation, what next? Could you escape instead?

One answer is: yes. But how? *Where* do you go? Can you outrun the pain threatening to consume you? You cannot return to yourself, your *half* of a self. If it wasn't enough before love, how could it possibly be enough now? And what if you were not simply searching for your other half before you found your beloved? What if you were trying to escape from yourself? There is an adage about not being able to run away from your problems, but what if you don't have to run? What if you don't need to make a geographical escape, but rather, an *artistic* one?

When reality proves to be painful and unsatisfying, art can offer an escape. Art can remake the world as you want to see it. Through the written word, through dance—through any artistic medium that transports you—you can be carried away from your broken heart. You *can* escape. This is the alternative the artist Salvador Dalí and the poet Federico García Lorca each felt best suited him when their intense, turbulent, and ultimately unresolved relationship left both men feeling vulnerable and alone.

For five years in the mid- to late 1920s, the two young men weaved together their realities and experienced the euphoria of being in love. And then, seemingly inevitably, came pain. How do you cope when the life you adored, the person you envisaged your future with, ceases to be a part of you, and you a part of them? Federico García Lorca was a broken man after the dissolution of his relationship with Dalí. Their fusion had been so powerful that Lorca could not envision the future without his beloved. It was a "place" where he did not want to find himself. He wanted to remain in the period of his life that has come to be known as his "Dalinian" years— but those had brutally come to an end. What then? Unable to make sense of his agony, he turned to poetry to overcome his grief. The reality of his life was too heart wrenching to engage with, so he reconstructed his world in words.

I began this chapter with Plato's conception of oneness because of its immense impact on Lorca's understanding of love. In his most painful year, 1928, the poet returned to the *Symposium*—which he had read in his youth—and lamented the impossibility of achieving wholeness: "Si el uno es la perfecta fusión de dos mitades, me decía, los hombres somos selvas de mitades en eterna busca de la imposible union" ("If one is the perfect fusion of two halves … then we men are jungles of halves eternally in search of the impossible union," he told his friend and confidante Rafael Martínez Nadal.[42] The impossibility of the union was only underscored by the powerful illusion of wholeness that he had felt with Dalí.

A "jungle": it is a forbidding place, disorienting, and full of danger at every turn. Yet there you are, searching, desperately yearning for that which completes you. You are moving *toward* something, the unknown that you are convinced will make you whole, will realize you fully.

On Dalí's side, the heartbreak was no less intense. Despite overt displays of bravado and distancing himself from Lorca and their affair, Dalí did not emerge unscathed. His engagement with surrealism, although not defined by his break from Lorca, can certainly be said to have been heavily informed by it. After all, when traditional modes of interpretation for emotions fail us, when the comforting assurance of oneness leaves us, what are we left with?

# RESIDENCIA DE ESTUDIANTES

The friendship Lorca and Dalí shared has mystified scholars for decades. We only partially know the story of the affair, because the majority of the letters Dalí wrote to Lorca—there were nearly forty—have never been found. Ana María, Dalí's sister, assumed they had been lost in the chaos of two world wars, but Dalí revealed in 1978 that he still had them in his possession and that at the right moment, he would make them public. This has, as of yet, not been done, and they don't form part of the Fundación Gala-Salvador Dalí in Figueres, where the artist's archives are held.

The love story began in the spring of 1923, when Lorca and Dalí first met at the famed Residencia de Estudiantes in Madrid. On the surface, the two men appeared to be complete opposites, but the *coup de foudre* was undeniable. They were immediately fascinated with each other. Lorca, six years Dalí's senior, had settled in Spain's capital in 1919 and was a somewhat mythical figure amongst the students at the "Resi."[43] As the de facto leader of the group of intellectual twenty-somethings, Lorca was revered, admired, and sought out for his thoughts and opinions. The filmmaker Luis Buñel, at the time also a student at the Resi, exclaimed that Lorca was the finest human being he'd ever known: "He was his own masterpiece," Buñel declared. "Whether sitting at the piano imitating Chopin, improvising a pantomime, or acting out a scene from a play, he was irresistible."[44] Dali undoubtedly became equally, if not more, enchanted by Lorca's intellect and magnetism.

In his autobiography, Dalí conveyed his first impression of the dashing poet:

... the personality of Federico Garcia Lorca produced a tremendous impression on me. The poetic phenomenon in its entirety and *incarnate* presented itself before me suddenly made of flesh and bone, confused, injected with blood, viscous and sublime, quivering with a thousand fires of darkness and of subterranean biology, like all matter bestowed with the originality of its own form ... when I felt the incendiary and expansive form of the poetry of the great Federico rise in wild, ruffled flames I tried to stifle it with the olive branch of my premature anti-Faustian old age.[45]

This impression grew into a sense of inferiority before the dynamic poet:

I avoided Lorca and the group, which grew to be his group more and more. This was the culminating moment of his irresistible personal influence—and the only moment in my life when I thought I glimpsed the torture that envy can be. Sometimes we would be walking, the whole group of us, along El Paseo de la Castellana on our way to the café where we held our usual literary meetings, and where I knew Lorca would shine like a mad and fiery diamond. Suddenly, I would set off at a run, and no one would see me for three days.[46]

Dalí escaped. From what? From himself? Out of fear of inferiority? Out of fear that his infatuation with the estimable Lorca would not be reciprocated? Whatever the reason, and wherever he went, Dalí had to return. He had to find another escape from himself, an escape of the sort that he had been cultivating from the time he was a child, namely, being anything and anyone other than himself. Perhaps only Dalí could ultimately answer the question of why he felt the need to escape. Yet there is ample evidence suggesting that he was an extremely shy boy who did not know how to be with others without carrying out a role, a persona.

The gravity of Dalí's reaction to Lorca was unique for Dalí. Here, after all, was a young man who'd thought himself a prodigy with boundless ambition and talent: "At the age of six I wanted to be a cook. At seven I wanted to be Napoleon. And my ambition has been growing steadily ever since."[47] Dalí had created his first oil painting at the young age of six, had put together his first exhibition at a youthful fourteen, and had written his first novel at only sixteen. By the time he met Lorca in Madrid, he was certainly accomplished in his own right, but the spell of attraction led him to see Lorca as a divine figure embodying the spontaneity and charisma that Dalí saw himself as lacking. Despite his public flamboyance, Dalí was really a shy workaholic who hid in his room, furiously drawing. But despite his rejection of the company of others and his desire for solitude, he deeply craved to arouse the sort of admiration Lorca elicited in their contemporaries. He wanted others to be fascinated with him at all costs; this became a defining characteristic throughout the painter's life.

Though his early days in Madrid were imbued with a persistent misanthropy, Dalí was careful to project an image of mystery and allure. The artist from Catalunya was physically striking and fashioned himself a dandy: Tall and pale, with effeminate features and slicked black hair, he dressed in luxurious velvet coats, large hats, and leather pants that drew stares in the halls of the Residencia. Perhaps, as he himself maintained, his exhibitionism was a way of attracting the admiration of others. From the time he was a child, Dalí had dressed elaborately. Later in life, he carried around a set of bells that jingled as he strutted around—"How else would I be sure they would notice me?"[48] he must have quipped. In everything he did, Dalí paid careful attention to being Dalí, to being *other*, unusual, unique, arguably in no need of a complementing and completing half. Lorca was seduced by Dalí's enigmatic persona and sense of drama.

The friendship blossomed almost immediately. Soon after they met, Dalí gave Lorca one of his paintings. The two spent their days in Madrid engaged in *tertulias,* drawn-out gatherings in a café where they were engrossed by each other. Through conversations about literature, art, aesthetics, and meaning, their minds and hearts began to intertwine, each searching for completion in the other. On some occasions, Dalí would sit at the table across from Lorca, sketching away at his portrait. Their conversations would sometimes end in disagreement, but they always valued each other's opinions profoundly—as they would continue to do for years following the dissolution of their friendship. In the other, it seems, each found the completion of his best self.

It is not surprising that powerful personalities and intellects such as Dalí's and Lorca's would form such an intense relationship. And though there has been considerable speculation about the exact nature of the friendship between the two men, there is no doubt that they loved each other deeply for several years, however that love may have expressed itself. Their relationship proved to be one of the most fruitful in twentieth-century Spanish arts and letters, but it was also a profoundly tender encounter in which both Lorca and Dali seemed to have found a kindred spirit.

## SEXUALITY VS. INTELLECTUAL INTIMACY

Lorca was tortured by his homosexuality and by a culture that despised, denigrated, feared, and denounced it.[49] He could not live publicly as a celebrated writer who happened to be homosexual. Raised as a Catholic, Lorca had to conceal his sexuality from his family and, later, from a public that admired his writing. He continued to attend mass throughout his life, which served as a constant reminder of what he considered his shame. Dalí did not seem to share his dear friend's torment. During his second Cadaques sojourn with the Dalí family, for example, Lorca attended mass on Sundays with Dalí's sister, Ana María, and immersed himself in the comfort of familiar rituals and phrases, as if washing away half of his real identity. Dalí, on the other hand, famously described himself as "profoundly anti-religious."[50]

A unified whole would perhaps have looked more like Plato's virtuous soul, a self whose parts harmonize in such a way that reason directs their activities. Of course, Plato's view practically disparages all things non- or irrational, but the principle of unity applies nonetheless. There is no reason to believe that if Lorca had allowed himself to be true to his sexuality in a traditional family, a Catholic society and a conservative country, the other aspects of his self would have been negatively affected. As Gema Pérez-Sánchez has noted, if Lorca had been allowed to be true to his sexuality, he would have lived in a world where his love poetry was not banned or censored for over twenty years because of its homoerotic overtones.[51] If he had been allowed to be true to his sexuality, he would not have had to bear the shame and self-hatred expected of a "deviant" in his beloved faith.

Sexual suppression found an outlet in both men's work, but it manifested in different ways. Given that sex itself was considered sinful outside of marriage, surely *homosexual* sex was entirely forbidden. Lorca's homosexuality added further complexity to his poetry, for it brought out elements of the theme the impossibility of fulfilling desire—a theme that, on some level, he poured into his writing.

If we return for a moment to Plato's proposal that love is a search for one's lost other half, perhaps we can apply the same principle within an individual. For Lorca was forced to divide himself, hiding one part in order to exist in a world that would not abide it. Indeed, he was even divided against himself, as his faith and society effectively demanded. Lorca was conflicted to some degree during the years when he was closest to Dalí, and he struggled to suppress his growing love for the artist.[52] To add salt to his wounds, Lorca's younger sister Concha became engaged around this time to Manuel Fernandez-Montesinos, a medical student and friend of Lorca's, and his brother Paquito was excelling academically at Oxford.[53] In September 1926, he wrote to his friend and fellow poet, Jorge Guillen: "Imagine that I would like to get married. Could I do that? No. And this is what I would like to resolve. I'm beginning to see that my heart seeks a garden and a small fountain as in my earliest poems."[54] Here was a young man yearning for a life that would never become a reality. He romanticized the idea of a simple life amidst "a garden and a little fountain," but he was split in two, for he knew he would never achieve this. Could this be why he—and Dalí—used sewing imagery in some of their work? Was each hoping to weave himself into a complete self?

In "The Gypsy Nun", a poem from Lorca's *Romancero Gitano*,[55] the poetic subject, the gypsy nun, represents an oxymoron—the desire for liberty and her state of moral repression. Her existence is confined and limited, and her only form of expression is through artistic creation. Within her enclosed surroundings, she embroiders "alhelíes," colourful flowers that are symbols of eroticism and sensuality, and "malvas," flowers that are commonly associated with mourning, onto a sacred cloth. Could this be a reflection of Lorca's predicament—the tug of war between reality and fantasy, repression and desire? The nun's religious dedication meant that she could only express her sexuality mentally and artistically—as sexual fantasies that were far from her more sobering reality. The poem is undoubtedly a commentary on the societal pressures and religious doctrines that stifle individuality and true expression.

The limited expression of sexuality and desire that Lorca depicts can help us understand the physical boundaries that came to characterize the relationship between the two men. In their love letters, poems, and paintings, they expressed unrivalled closeness, despite the fact that Dalí maintained that he had rebuffed his dear friend Lorca's sexual advances and that their romance was never actually consummated!

Those who knew both the poet and the artist—Pepin Bello, Luis Buñuel, and Rafael Martinez Nadal—suggested, as Dalí himself often did, that Dalí was embellishing the truth. Buñuel went so far as to describe Dalí as the "asexual" cerebral Apollonian force in the friendship, while Lorca was the Dionysian, earthly, sensual energy that grounded them. Yet one quick glance at Dalí's paintings will quickly contradict this; his paintings from the mid- to late 1920s are characterized by an abundance of genitalia, phallic objects, severed hands, and rotting female torsos amidst hidden representations of Lorca, depicted as a decapitated head with closed eyes. Might the head's detachment from the body possibly be a symbol that Dalí was comfortable with their mental and emotional closeness, but not with physical closeness?

What Dalí's art also reveals is that, at least on some level, Dalí reciprocated his friend's advances. In a photograph taken during their idyllic stay in Cadaques, Lorca and Dalí can be seen sitting across from each other at a table that shows the spontaneity and fun that characterized their time together. The cord of Lorca's bathrobe is stretched across the table between their two foreheads, connecting them, as if they are transmitting thoughts back and forth. Indeed, Dalí later wrote that at this time, "for the duration of an eclipse," Lorca darkened the "virginal originality of my spirit and of my flesh"[56]—he also felt that two were becoming one.

In her biography of Lorca, Leslie Stainton writes that by the spring of 1925, the two were inseparable companions:

They made several weekend excursions to Toledo and in March, they took a trip to the mountains north of Madrid. Each found in the other a reflection of his own beliefs and ambitions and, most of all, talent. There was an element of idolatry to their friendship, of mutual awe, but also, increasingly, of love. They understood each other in ways no one else did or could, and as time wore on, they came to need one another with growing urgency.[57]

Their devotion to each other was cemented when Lorca spent Easter week in Catalunya with the Dalí family. They found themselves at their most inspired and creative in those few blissful days together, and their weekly letters immediately following Lorca's return to Granada show a nearly obsessive back-and-forth correspondence filled with cryptic, homoerotic references.[58]

No doubt, there were two sides to each man, so that it was not simply the case that they were each other's long-lost half—although a proposal of Lorca's does explain at least some of the intensity in their relationship: "Let us agree that one of man's most beautiful postures is that of Saint Sebastian," Lorca once said.[59] Lorca's own poetry hails the early Christian saint and martyr, and Dalí's painting of the young man shot through with arrows expresses the tensions that made up the Dalí–Lorca romance. Nevertheless, short-lived though their relationship was, Lorca and Dalí were indeed exemplars of the idea that you can meet someone who fits you. You just belong together from the very start, and it is as if you've always been this way.

Although their sexuality may have complicated their relationship, there is no doubt that sex was not its defining feature. How could it have been, after all, when the sheer brilliance of each man could not be limited to sexuality? As Dalí swooned in a letter to Lorca, "What are you up to? What are you working on? Please don't stop writing. You're the only interesting man I've ever met."[60] Theirs was a love affair that may have involved sexual desire; however, to extend the foundation Plato set in the story of the hermaphrodites, it went far beyond the body. Perhaps their love was the only true love that can ever be felt—that which is never fully experienced because it is not consummated by the body. Three years before his death, Dalí reflected on his friendship with Lorca: "It was an erotic and tragic love, because of the fact that it could not be shared."[61]

If true, this would likely also have compounded Lorca's distress over a deep, yet ultimately unsatisfying romance—a romance in which each was perfect for the other in all ways but one. Indeed, Dalí was apparently not a particularly physical person. He didn't like to be touched, so his alleged rejection of his dear friend would not be a surprising reality. That, of course, does not mean that Dalí did not have homosexual tendencies, even if he married Gala,[62] a woman with whom he collaborated over the years following his breakup with Lorca.

*Venus and Sailor (Homage to Salvat-Papasseit)* is perhaps Dalí's best expression of his sexual ambivalence from the Resi period. Dalí's rendition of Venus adheres, for instance, to classical forms and is reminiscent of Botticelli's iconic

Venus. The goddess of love's flowing golden tresses, crimson lips, tilted visage, and alabaster skin are all present in Dalí's work. But Dali has teleported her into the twentieth century. Rather than standing on a shell, Venus is sitting on the lap of a faceless sailor who also happens to be one-dimensional. This suggestion of sexual intimacy is altogether missing from the older work. Rather than floating over the water in an otherworldly style, Dalí's Venus is inside a room with a balcony that overlooks the sea. This setting makes her appear far more tangible and accessible than her famous predecessor, and yet the incongruence between the luscious Venus and the flat sailor dissolves any hope of erotic play between them.

Boticelli's Venus exists only in the two-dimensional image. Dalí, on the other hand, illustrates the limitations of sensorial experience not just by giving her a would-be, one-dimensional lover, but also by confining Venus in a room framed by black, vertical slabs that shut out the outside world while leaving space for a view that verifies the existence of something beyond the confines of the black frames. Dalí's Venus leaves us with a disarming sense of uncertainty. The image of Venus is familiar and should put us at ease, but instead it causes confusion. We think we recognize her, but we're not sure why. She appears, somehow, to be out of place.

This is one instance of a type of physical and emotional distancing that recurs in Dalí's work, and it just might be indicative of his own internal struggles with connecting so completely with another human being. If one finds one's so-called other half, but is somehow unable to truly and completely connect with that person, then one must be profoundly bereft. Reality is messy, and, it would seem, so was the friendship between Lorca and Dalí—complicated, in any event, by their individual tribulations. Curiously enough, and perhaps compounding the difficulties in their relationship, Lorca and Dalí both manifested emotional detachment or dehumanization in their work, but in different ways. Lorca's work reflected the holistic experience of sense perception, and his systematic imagery—moon, blood, water, horse and rider, for example—emphasize that focus. Dalí, on the other hand, wanted to take common objects and reduce them to their individual parts. He rejected sentimentality and symbolism and preferred to focus on more cerebral topics and a sort of intellectual dissonance.

# The Rupture

Why does rejection hurt so much? Being told by someone you are in love with that you are no longer satisfying them, no longer the source of their happiness, is a crushing thing to hear—regardless of how sweetly or logically it is said to you. It reinforces in us the thought that beneath it all, we are the unlovable, wretched little monsters we fear of being at our very core. Rejection is a judgement passed on our entire being—mental, physical, and emotional. How do we retain our self-worth after such a letdown as this? A person we have opened up to, one with whom we have experienced indescribable intimacy that no one else can ever understand, has decided that we are no longer what they want—they have seen the depths of our soul and concluded: "This is not for me." When we stand at the epicenter of heartbreak, the saddest words can be, as Elton John wrote, "I'm sorry."

Regarding Dalí and Lorca, the events that led to their rupture are not entirely clear. We do know that Lorca abruptly and hastily left Cadaques, where he had been a guest of Dalí's. From a café in Barcelona, he wrote to his beloved Salvador:

> I want to cry... I've behaved like an indecent donkey with you... you, who are the best thing there is for me. As the minutes go by I see it clearly and I am truly remorseful. Yet this only increases my affection for you and my attachment to your way of thinking and your human quality.[63]

He did not elaborate further on what had caused him to leave; he only requested that Dalí put his name on the artist's latest painting so that the name Federico García Lorca "might amount to something in the world." Lorca wrote again to Dalí:

> I think of you and of your little house. I've never thought more intensely than now. I am at my limit. I hope you'll write me... And that you'll tell me if you resent me or if you've erased me from your friendships.[64]

And again:

> I think of you always. I think of you too much. I feel as though I am holding a hot gold coin in my hand and I cannot let go of it. But also, I don't want to let go of it *little son*. I have to imagine that you are hideously ugly in order to love you more.[65]
> If only ceasing to love another were so simple—but the bonds of love are (for better and sometimes for worse) far more interweaved than merely on a physical level.

How can we interpret these letters? As the year progressed, Dalí began to write less and less; he was busy with his tour of duty in the army and planning his first exhibition in Paris. While we can't establish a concrete ending to the relationship between Dali and Lorca, we know that the relationship had severely deteriorated by the end of 1928. From that time on, a newfound hostility can be sensed in Dalí's estimation of Lorca and his influence. The following year, Dali officially associated himself with the surrealist movement.

Clearly, there were not only differences between the two friends; there were also internal fractures within each of them. García Lorca was tormented by the two lives he was forced to live: one as the celebrated poet, and the other as the hidden homosexual. He was an avant-garde poet and play-wright, but also a devotee of traditionalist storytelling and Spanish folklore. For his part, Dalí struggled between shy-ness and exhibitionism. The questions abound: How, if at all, did Lorca's homosexuality and Dalí's public rejection of the rumours about an affair impact them? Why was the exhibi-tionist Dalí adamant about his heterosexuality? Dalí, known to hate being physically touched, married Gala. Was this a rebuke to Lorca?

Dalí's coldness towards Lorca led the poet to escape into a "rebound" relationship, with a twenty-one year old sculp-tor from Madrid who had an uncanny resemblance to Dalí. Emilio Aladrén was clearly not Lorca's intellectual equal, as Dalí had been, but he idolized Lorca, and the poet cherished the attention following his heartbreak with Dalí. About to turn thirty, Lorca was easily seduced by Aladrén's youth and beauty in the spring and summer of 1928, but as is often the case with rebounds, Aladrén was no replacement for the original. Lorca confessed to his old roommate José Antonio

Rubio Sacristán from his Residencia days: "I've been through (I'm going through) one of the most profound crises of my life." He continued:

It's my poetic destiny. We cannot gamble with what life and blood gives us, because we become enchained when we least desire it. I now realize what it is that the erotic poets mean by the fire of love, and I have come to this realization precisely when I need to cut it from my life in order not to go under... You had never seen me so bitter, and it's true. Now I am full of despair, with no wish for anything, crippled. This makes me feel extraordinarily humble. We'll see if I can achieve what I desire with my poetry, we'll see if I can finally cut these terrible bonds and return to my happiness, to my old happiness, a breastplate against bitterness.[66]

Critics have associated these lines with Aladrén, but do they not seem to actually refer to Dalí? It certainly could be the case. Lorca wrote to the Colombian poet Jorge Zalamea: "I'm going through one of the most painful periods I've experienced in my life."[67] He also wrote to Rafael Martínez Nadal: "Don't get involved with anyone, Rafael. It's better to be cruel with others and not to have to suffer calvary, passion, and death afterward... It's a sad fact that the blows a poet receives are the seed of his work, his ladder of light."[68] For the third summer in a row, he had implored Dalí to visit him in Granada, but Dalí never did make it back to the south to see Lorca. Lorca spent the following months in a daze of depression. To make matters worse, Dali began collaborating on a script with Buñuel, who had grown increasingly hostile towards Lorca. For his part, Lorca felt as though he was being replaced.

Dalí was also struggling internally with his life post-Lorca, the tremendous momentum his artistic success gained in these years. He later admitted that he experienced a "self-destructive rage" in the 1920s. For example, he defaced a painting of the Sacred Heart, writing on it "Sometimes I spit for pleasure on the portrait of my mother." In reaction to this, Dalí's father and sister broke off all ties with him. Dalí's father wrote to Lorca upon hearing about Dalí's antics:

I do not know if you already know that I have had to throw my son out of the house. He's a disgrace, an ignoramus, and an unrivalled pedant, in addition to being a perfect rascal. He thinks he knows everything, and yet he doesn't even know how to read and write. In short, you know him better than I do.[69]

Dalí was clearly acting out. The rupture of Dali's relationship with Lorca may have been his first romantic heartbreak, but he had known the ache of a broken heart from before. Dalí's brother and aunt both died when he was just a boy. The worst blow, however, came in 1921, when Dalí was only fifteen years old: his mother died of uterine cancer at the age of forty-seven. Dalí was devastated. In his autobiography, *The Secret Life of Salvador Dalí,* he said that his mother's death "was the greatest blow I had experienced in my life. I worshipped her... I could not resign myself to the loss of a being on whom I counted to make invisible the unavoidable blemishes of my soul."[70] Having been seen so clearly yet lovingly by another person—and then having that person abruptly disappear—must have set quite a challenge for anyone who later encountered Dalí.

It's not unusual for tragedy and death to force us into contemplation and to spark new ideas, and this first pain may have been the push Dalí needed for escaping his hometown and venturing into the heart of Spain to begin his formal studies. In Dali's diaries from May of 1920, he already expresses the joy of painting itself as a form of escape:

As soon as I was ready, I opened the cupboard in my room and carefully took out some boxes. I opened them. They had the tubes of paint. Those clean and shiny tubes represented for me a whole world of aspirations, and I looked at them and caressed them with hands trembling with emotions, just as I imagine lovers do, and I saw my tubes emptying their pure colors onto the palette, and my brushes catching them up lovingly. I saw my work progressing. The suffering in creation. My ecstasy as I lost myself in the mystery of light, of colour, of life… more light, more blue… more sun… losing myself in Nature, being her submissive disciple… oh, I could go mad![71]

Both the poet and the artist would have to turn to poetry and art to overcome their feelings of anguish, to lose themselves, to escape. But how they sought escape would prove different for Lorca and Dalí.

## Lorca's Crisis of Identity: The Futility of Finding Yourself by Escaping from Pain

Reality following a traumatic breakup can seem too much to handle. You want to close your eyes, shut down your mind, and cease to feel in your heart, because the pain is too much to bear. Heartbreak produces a throbbing, sharp sensation that cannot be ignored. It consumes you. Healing takes time, but in your grief you cannot even imagine yourself healed or whole again. You are broken. What if you cannot be fixed? What if you simply cannot wait, as every passing second is an agonizing reminder of all you have lost and the emptiness that lies ahead?

It is not uncommon to simply want to escape. Romantic films and songs all talk about pulling down the blinds, hiding under your covers, and hoping that the world disappears—or even better yet, that you disappear from it.

Lorca and Dalí have a lot to say about escapism, at least in terms of their actions and their art—and we have a lot to learn from them in this regard, both positive and negative. The writer and artist offer us two forms of escape that could prove helpful to you in the aftermath of a breakup. The first is Lorca's escape, which took him out of his wallowing, self-absorption and thrust him outwards. By developing empathy and a social conscience, Lorca transformed his own ache into poetry that came to be a powerful vehicle for change.

The months following his distancing from Dalí were excruciating for Lorca. He later described this as a time during which he underwent a "penumbra sentimental,"[72] an emotional crisis. For seven months following his composition of the *Poemas en prosa* (*Poems in Prose*), he did not write a word. He needed to get away from Spain—to physically escape—and he decided to go to New York with the pretext of studying at Columbia University.

Escaping Spain allowed Lorca to affirm his worth. From the boat that took him across the Atlantic, he wrote, "But… forward! No matter how insignificant I may be, I believe that I *deserve* to be loved."[73] But his recognition that he was a being deserving of love and care did not end his crisis. No sooner did he proclaim "Onward!" than he begin to doubt. For during this same voyage, he wrote a letter questioning why he had even left Spain: "I don't know why I left. I ask myself that question a hundred times a day. I look at myself in the mirror of the confining cabin and I don't recognize myself. I seem to be another Federico."[74] Lorca's self-crisis poured over into his early poetry in New York, with an alienated, fragmented sense of self struggling to emerge from the rubble.

The surrealist George Bataille wrote that "only the poet's interminable agony can really reveal the authenticity of poetry."[75] That may be true, but only creativity can provide an outlet for the overbearing sense of anguish and despair that an artist experiences as a result of heartbreak. What emerges in Lorca's early New York poems is a picture of a man on a journey of self-discovery—or rediscovery—after having seemingly lost himself in his pain. But aren't the very concepts of "losing" and "finding" oneself rather odd? What exactly does it mean to "find oneself," and how exactly ought we to go about it? In our culture, this phrase is often used without giving it much thought, but we must be able to define it if we are to ever understand it. If we talk about losing and finding ourselves, we are assuming that somewhere out there is our real, authentic self, just waiting for us to uncover it—just as our other half was waiting for us to find him or her before we fell in love. The idea that we can "find" this enigmatic self rests on the incorrect assumption that out there is an unchanging, permanent "essence," a what it is to be you, that only needs discovering.

But what does that render the self who is searching? What does it do to the you who is aching, confused, and fragmented? Is *that* not really "you"? It is comforting to live with the illusion that once we succeed in finding ourselves, we will lead happy lives, filled with purpose and meaning, just as we thought that once we met our other half, we would be complete. The illusion is that our despair is only the cause of us being "lost," just as we were before we met our beloved. Yes, this is merely an illusion. When Lorca peers into the abyss (the "huecos," or holes, that he so often refers to in his New York poems), what stares back at him is emptiness. Lorca's vision has been described as "apocalyptic"—there is an all-pervading sense of alienation, dehumanization, and hostility in the early New York poems. Old modes of understanding the self no longer make sense in the angst and despair the poetic voice experiences, and this leads him to question himself, his existence, and his place in the world.

The first poem of the collection, "Vuelta de paseo" ("After a Walk"), sets up the poet's resignation in the face of absurdity:

Asesinado por el cielo,
entre las formas que van hacia la sierpe
y las formas que buscan el cristal,
dejaré crecer mis cabellos
(Assassinated by the sky,
between forms moving towards the serpent
and forms searching for the crystal,
I'll let my hair grow).

Have we not all felt this after a breakup—albeit perhaps in not such poetic terms? Our attitude is passive: we cannot make a decision, we cannot exercise our will, we cannot make an effort. We are passive victims of our fate and meaning is impossible, so we will just step back and let ourselves be assassinated. The assassination here is of the spiritual self, not the physical self, and it happens to the poet regardless of his desire. In short, he is a victim. This passivity is further expressed by Lorca's resignation to letting his hair grow, much as it continues to grow on a corpse following death.

The poem that follows in the collection, titled "1910," is an elegiac look back in time to the poet's childhood, at age twelve, before he experienced the pain and cruelty of adult life. Here Lorca reflects upon his past and laments an innocence that has been lost:

Aquellos ojos míos de mil novecientos diez no vieron enterrar a los muertos, ni la feria de ceniza del que llora por la madrugada, ni el corazón que tiembla arrinconado como un caballito de mar.

Aquellos ojos míos de mil novecientos diez vieron la blanca pared donde orinaban las niñas, el hocico del toro, la seta venenosa y una luna incomprensible que iluminaba por los rincones los pedazos de limón seco bajo el negro duro de las botellas.

Aquellos ojos míos en el cuello de la jaca, en el seno traspasado de Santa Rosa dormida, en los tejados del amor, con gemidos y frescas manos, en un jardín donde los gatos se comían a las ranas.

Desván donde el polvo viejo congrega estatuas y musgos, cajas que guardan silencio de cangrejos devorados en el sitio donde el sueño tropezaba con su realidad. Allí mis pequeños ojos.

No preguntarme nada. He visto que las cosas cuando buscan su curso encuentran su vacío. Hay un dolor de huecos por el aire sin gente y en mis ojos criaturas vestidas ¡sin desnudo!

(Those eyes of mine in nineteen-ten
saw no one dead and buried,

no village fair of ash from the one who weeps at
dawn,
no trembling heart cornered like a seahorse.

Those eyes of mine in nineteen-ten
saw the white wall where little girls pissed,
the bull's muzzle, the poisonous mushroom,
and an incomprehensible moon illuminating dried
lemon rinds
under the hard black bottles in corners.

Those eyes of mine on the pony's neck,
on the pierced breast of Santa Rosa as she sleeps,
on the rooftops of love, with moans and cool hands,
on a garden where cats devour frogs.

Attic where the ancient dust assembles statues and
moss.
Boxes that keep the silence of devoured crabs.
In the place where the dream was colliding with its
reality.
My little eyes are there.

Don't ask me any questions. I've seen how things
that seek their way find their void instead.
There are spaces that ache in the uninhabited air
and in my eyes, completely dressed creatures—no
one naked there!)

The poet cannot reconcile his former self with his present self—those eyes from 1910 are no longer the same eyes through which he sees the world nearly two decades later. The innocence with which he once saw both death and sexuality had now long been lost, along with countless objects that, by the time he arrived in New York, had found their place in the attic of his past.

The past as an attic where memories and objects get stored, where "the dream was colliding with reality," is an interesting concept in the context of losing and hoping to find oneself. But perhaps the most intriguing bit of the poem is the final stanza, in its most emotive line, "I've seen how things that seek their way find their void instead." This certainly brings to mind Kierkegaard's take on self-reflection: "What did I find? Not my 'I', for that is exactly what I was trying in that way to find (I imagined, if I may so put it, my soul shut up in a box with a spring lock in front, which the external surroundings would release by pressing the spring)."[76]

Like Kierkegaard before him, Lorca rejects the idea that there is somewhere a self in a box waiting to pop out and surprise him. Lorca cannot find himself because there is no "self" separate from him that he can observe. No, he must *create* himself, and this requires being present, not escaping. There must have been a moment when Lorca realized that selfhood isn't something a person automatically has; selfhood begins where victimization ends. A human being can spend an entire lifetime not being a self, but instead just existing: eating, sleeping, having sex, eliminating bladders and bowels.

But to merely exist on autopilot is just that: to merely exist. Whether you want to have a pulse and continue to "be" in this world is not really up to you, at least insofar as you are here. You have found yourself. HERE. The *way* you live is entirely up to you. As Kierkegaard reminds us, it's not the *what* of belief that matters, it's the *how*.[77] How will you be in the world? How will you confront the self that is not in a box but there, in the mirror, in every thought you think?

Following a breakup, you don't *find* yourself. You must carefully, consciously, and thoughtfully decide who you are and who you want to be, and then work towards that with everything in you. The self begins when you acknowledge yourself to yourself and take responsibility for your actions *as yours*.

For Lorca, this meant readjusting the zoom of his internal camera away from himself, to others. Lorca had always had a social conscience, and perhaps the introspection and indulgent melancholy he experienced following his personal setbacks with Dalí led to him to feel that he had "lost" himself. By turning his gaze back to the plights of others he saw the same loss of innocence and degradation in society that he first identified in himself.

Lorca's escape, therefore, consisted in turning outwards. He saw in America the mindless activity that consists of existing as a human but not living as a self. Heidegger described the "average everydayness": a mode of being that consists of living unreflectively, complacently, in a mundane reality. Heidegger (and Lorca) saw this as an inauthentic, or fallen, state, in which we have an unquenchable thirst for distractions. This, Heidegger believed, limits us as individuals and proves to be a barrier between a person and the realization of that person's "self." In searching for our so-called self, we ignore our own embodiment and abandon the self that is there before us. In looking for the "I" in a box, a soul or spirit hiding within us that is our *true*, our *real* self, we overlook what it is to be us, right now, in this moment, where we are continually generating ourselves right under our own noses—deliberating, choosing, creating. In merely existing, we ignore the self we carry with us. We do not even bother to seek. We are not this way or that way. We just are.

In a lecture that Lorca often delivered between 1931 and 1935, titled "A Poet in New York," he observed:

At first sight, the rhythm may seem to be joyful, but when you look more closely at the mechanism of social life and the painful slavery of men and machines, you see it as a typical empty anguish in comparison with which crime and banditry are a forgivable means of evasion....

Lorca lamented the pleasure-seeking masses at Coney Island in the poem "Paisaje de la multitude que vomita" ("Landscape of a Vomiting Multitude"), which appears as a nightmarish vision.

Coney Island is a great fair where every Sunday in the summer more than a million creatures come. They drink, they shout, they eat, they writhe about leaving a sea full of newspapers and streets littered with tin cans, cigarette butts, bites of food and shoes with broken heels.

No one can imagine the loneliness a Spaniard feels there; because if you fall you will be trampled and if you slide into the water, they will throw lunch wrappers on you.[78]

Is this not what Heidegger's "average everydayness" means? Is this not what it means to be blind to who we are and who we could choose to be?

Wall Street and its preoccupation with money were even more upsetting to Lorca:

The terrible, cold and cruel part is Wall Street. Rivers of gold flow there from every part of the world, accompanied by death. There, as in no other place, one finds a total absence of spirit: herds of men who cannot count past three; herds more who cannot count past six, who scorn pure science and madly worship only the present. And the terrible thing is that the people who fill the street are convinced that the world will always be the same, and that they are obliged to keep the machine running day in, day out.[79]

# The Illusion of Escape: Hedonism, Stoicism, and Skepticism Respond to Psychic Pain

If we turn once again to ancient thinkers, we find several ways in which each man could be said to have attempted escape, first the escape from himself, before the friendship, and then from the emotional devastation after the breakup. Three schools of thought from the Hellenistic period, Epicureanism, stoicism, and skepticism, share a common feature: a belief that the good life is free from emotional disturbance. Clearly, the agony of heartbreak was not merely a disturbance for each man, but an emotional cataclysm. At first blush, these philosophies, so different in important respects, would seem perfect for one who is seeking escape. It is attractive to think that one could escape the torment of emotional destruction. Who would not want to be free from the stabbing, relentless ache of heartbreak? Upon closer examination, however, we find that freedom from disturbance does not equate escape. In fact, it's the opposite.

Epicurus flourished in Athens in the third century BCE. He admired the atomists, who believed that reality consists of an infinite number of material particulates that move, collide, and conglomerate in an infinite void and have no divinely inspired meaning. The gods, busy with their own affairs, did not interfere in the lives of men. Consequently, we should not be concerned with them. Instead, our lives should be aimed at the highest good, pleasure. However, this does not mean, for example, eating or drinking to excess, because the subsequent pain is greater than the short-lived pleasure. Additionally, intensity in pleasure or pain is a disturbance. If we want proper pleasure, Epicurus holds, we should live a life of moderation in all things.

The stoics, while disagreeing with the hedonists about the gods and pleasure, held an entirely deterministic view of the universe. Things happen according to a divine plan; there is no deviating from it; and since it's ultimately a divine plan, it's a good one. Our only option for a peaceful state of mind and happy life is to give up what we cannot control, such as our social status, physical limitations, and so forth, and align our emotions with what is. One stoic famously admonishes a parent whose child has died to declare the death to be nothing.

Finally, the ancient skeptics doubted that knowledge claims based on sense perception could be verified as objectively true. The basic problem, they claimed, is that knowledge claims based on sense perception can conflict with each other ("This sauce is spicy!" "What? No, it's not. You can barely taste the heat."). There is no objective measure whereby such inconsistencies can be resolved. What we can do, rather, is to suspend judgment about what appears to us. This allows us a type of mental calm or tranquility that we would not achieve otherwise.

In each case, the philosophers sought to reconcile themselves with the world around them, not to escape it. The right sort of attitude, the right sort of disposition allows us to truly live, to robustly live—not to escape. Freedom is not, on this general view of things, equivalent to escape; it is the same as running from oneself or one's heartbreak. Coming to understand how things are allows us not to be troubled when otherwise, we would be. Clearly, however, Dalí and Lorca, each in his own way, did not come to terms with himself or his relation with his dear friend.

CHAPTER 3

―――――

YOU AWAKEN TO FIND YOUR lover has vanished. Without warning. Without notice. Only the night before, an arm was draped across your body. Familiar, accustomed, natural. Was there a word, a gesture you missed? What went wrong? Why would he leave with no explanation? How could your lover disappear as if he had never existed? Nothing makes sense. Meaning and comfort have fallen away like autumn leaves. You are alone. You are bereft. You are inconsolable. And you are trapped in this moment—this *eternal now*. There is no healing with time because there *is* no time. There is only an ever-present ache where once there was joy. There is only silence in the space your beloved once occupied.

Heartbreak is intimate, deeply subjective, entirely singular, and yet also universal. In those first moments of bewilderment, of slowly dawning realization, we're frozen in time. *What now? Where do we turn? How can we move on?* The answers to these questions are as singular as heartbreak itself.

But what if we choose to be enriched by this moment, even as we wish it weren't real?

We can find clues for how to do this in philosophy, art, and Greek mythology. Instead of being victims of heartbreak, we're about to look at this common human experience through a philosophical lens that reveals our inner strengths. For this journey, we'll stand on the shoulders of giants in philosophy and art. Through the insights of Friedrich Nietzsche, the nineteenth-century philosopher and author, and Giorgio de Chirico, the twentieth-century painter, we'll see that heartbreak can open us to the fullness of life with all of its inherent pleasures and pains, gains, and losses. Nietzsche's philosophy and de Chirico's paintings inspire us to create our own meaning by embracing and overcoming suffering.

Nietzsche's perspective is founded on the concept of "life affirmation." He embraced the reality of this world and didn't spend much time thinking about the world beyond. His philosophy champions our creative powers to strive beyond social, cultural, and moral contexts.[80]

De Chirico mirrors Nietzsche's philosophy and conveys it through paintings rather than words: His artwork is philosophy transferred to a canvas. An Italian who grew up in Greece, de Chirico created a series of paintings depicting the Greek myth of Ariadne. The paintings show Ariadne *immediately before* and *immediately after* she realizes that her beloved has abandoned her. Her despair and emptiness are palpable, but we also sense her underlying strength.

Both Nietzsche and de Chirico were deeply influenced by the Greeks and the Ariadne myth, in particular. They placed a high value on the Greeks' ferociously expressed humanity. The Greeks defined tragedy *and* triumph. Only their epic suffering can equal their primordial, full embrace of life—indeed, these are inseparable. According to Nietzsche, the Greek response to the horror and suffering of human life is not to be paralyzed with fear, but rather to create life-affirming art, music, and dance. The Greek myths and plays teach us that life is messy and the gods are fickle, empathetic, petty, and vindictive, just like us. Through Nietzsche's and de Chirico's interpretations of the Ariadne myth, we can gain insight into creating meaning by embracing and overcoming suffering.

There are several versions of this Greek myth, but they all have certain elements in common. As the story goes, Ariadne was the young and beautiful daughter of Minos, the King of Crete, the largest Greek island. As a tribute to the god Apollo, Minos regularly sacrificed young men and women by sending them to wander in a twisting labyrinth until the minotaur, a bull-headed monster that lived in the maze, ate them. One day, a young Athenian man named "Theseus" decided he would sail to Crete to kill the minotaur and end the decades-long ritual of sacrifice. Ariadne fell in love with Theseus and assisted him in his quest to slay the minotaur and escape from the labyrinth. He succeeded, and they fled from the island together. On their way to Athens, they stopped at an island called Naxos. The following morning Ariadne discovered that her beloved, for whom she had sacrificed everything, was gone. Later, Dionysus, the Greek god of fertility and wine, discovered Ariadne and married her.

While marrying a god may sound like the happiest ending ever, it didn't erase the suffering that Ariadne endured when Theseus abandoned her. This suffering becomes a focal point in de Chirico's Ariadne series. His portrayals of her provide a point of entry for discussing his view of suffering and the influence that Nietzsche's thought had on de Chirico's art. The parallels between the art, the artist, and theory lead us to a philosophical view of heartbreak and how we can come to accept it and use the energy of our intense emotions to create art and ultimately overcome our suffering.

# FINDING MEANING IN HEARTBREAK

Ariadne and her suffering serve as a link between De Chirico and Nietzsche because of their shared interest in her myth. In this combination we can find a recipe for creativity. De Chirico, as the main proponent of *Pittura Metafisica* (Metaphysical Painting), sought to create an experience of "revelation" through the enigmatic nature of his paintings. He didn't paint as a *painter*, but rather as a *philosopher*.

The description of de Chirico's paintings as "metaphysical" grants them a peculiar theoretical bent by connecting them to the branch of philosophy that's concerned with the nature of reality and what *is*. And for de Chirico, *what is* is fraught with melancholy, pensiveness, and a pervasive loneliness—all essential ingredients for existential ache. What better way to express the eternal moment than through the austerity that surrounds the voluptuous Ariadne in his paintings? The maiden, exquisitely primed for womanhood, her body blossoming with the *expectation of love* fulfilled, is not only abandoned, but in a cruel fashion in a foreign land. Unknown territory is bewildering, and Ariadne is quite literally lost until she finds her own inner compass.

The Ariadne myth is far from idyllic. Numerous artists have portrayed her as an *explicitly sexual* being, typically deep in slumber, unaware of her lover's betrayal. De Chirico's portrayals of Ariadne, on the other hand, consistently depict her at the enigmatic moment just before she becomes fully aware of her fate. Awakening from a deep sleep, which she had entered in the belief that she was united with her beloved, she is beginning to realize that all is lost. She then weeps in suffering over her lost love.

Theseus's actions do not seem *rational*. He demonstrates that it's not just the gods whose whims and meddling wreak havoc. Theseus's reason for leaving Ariadne—in what appeared to be cowardly manner—is a mystery. Perhaps he had a new lover; perhaps he worried about the scandal caused by bringing King Minos's daughter back to Athens; or perhaps Dionysus wanted Ariadne for himself and made Theseus forget his promise to Ariadne. In any case, the lack of meaning that can be attached to the abandonment is a crucial component of both de Chirico's and Nietzsche's interest in the story. De Chirico's work, when compared with that of his artistic contemporaries, shows a heightened awareness of the eternal questions: Who am I? Where did I come from? Why am I here? Where am I going? This awareness is underscored by a peculiar uncertainty regarding whether answers to these sorts of questions can ever be found. De Chirico credits both Nietzsche and Arthur Schopenhauer for teaching him "the non-sense of life" and its expression in art.[81]

In an early work, de Chirico painted a self-portrait that closely resembles a photograph taken of Nietzsche in 1882—as well as one of Schopenhauer. De Chirico's pose is that of melancholy. The philosophers' influence on the artist is obvious in this self-portrait. De Chirico posed as his primary intellectual hero Nietzsche did, with his chin resting sturdily on his left hand, his head turned slightly away from the viewer, and an expression that suggests immersion in thought and disconcertment. Indeed, it is through contemplation that one confronts one's melancholy. All subtlety is absent from the inscription beneath the portrait, which resonates with Nietzsche's thinking on the enigmatic nature of existence: "What shall I love if not the enigma?"

Ariadne's heart was broken by what was the epitome of enigma; Theseus's disappearance was puzzling and inexplicable. But all heartbreak is somewhat enigmatic. We may know exactly why our heart has broken, but our pervasive feeling is that it *just doesn't make sense*: Why doesn't he love me? How could she leave me?

Enigma evokes confusion, distress, and melancholy, even as it provokes *contemplation*. It's possible that these emotional states may be essential steps in the process of recovery. If we become mired in distress and fail to recover, then, in Nietzschean terms, we cannot truly affirm ourselves. Through visual art, literature, or pithy observations, we can witness de Chirico and Nietzsche attempt to evoke, solicit, or draw out the meaning of enigmatic heartbreak and its transformative power. As we waver on the brink of using that power, we may pull back. We may retreat from it exactly because of what it is. How many of us really want to know the truth about our heartbreak? Ariadne never knows why Theseus has abandoned her. She can fill this void however she wishes. She can call Theseus cruel and wallow in her righteous self-pity. She can excuse him by making up a reason that will also avert her own humiliation at having been left without a word. No matter how she decides to proceed, the unknown and *unknowable* are rich with sadness. The existential confrontation with enigma is agonizing. And as she drowsily becomes aware of her situation, *she* becomes the enigma, a human labyrinth.

It's possible that Nietzsche was drawn to the enigma because of his own familiarity with suffering, both physical and emotional. Born in Germany in 1844, Nietzsche experienced heartbreak before his fifth birthday, when his father died. A year later, one of his brothers died, and he was sent to his paternal grandparents' home, where he lived until he left for college. He went on to become a successful academic and was appointed to a professorship even before he completed his doctoral degree in philology. But he also became incapacitated by torturous migraines and a variety of ailments, such as stomach upsets of unknown origin (although some have suspicions about the cause)—and here again, we have mystery. He ultimately resigned his post as chair at Basel University when he was only thirty-four.

In addition to his physical problems, Nietzsche was devastated in love. His deep friendship with the composer Richard Wagner ended poorly when Wagner married the woman Nietzsche loved. Before that, Nietzsche's affair with Lou von Salomé, a young philosophy and theology student, ended when she took up with another good friend of his. These heartbreaks either caused or deepened his depression, and he withdrew from his family and friends. On January 3, 1889, while spending time in Turin, he experienced a mental breakdown which left him an invalid who spent the rest of his life in his sister's and mother's care.

Whether or not Nietzsche's philosophical views would have been very different had he experienced significant and sustained joy in his personal life is itself an enigma. But we do know that at least some of his philosophy reflected his on-going struggles. Whether a thinker's personal life is relevant for understanding his or her intellectual output is a matter of some debate, but Nietzsche did not separate his life from his thought. So it's not surprising that his interpretation of the Ariadne myth breaks with traditional artistic renderings in at least two important ways. For one thing, he focuses on Ariadne as a heroine. He does not understand her as a victim of heartbreak in traditionally chauvinistic terms, whereby she can be made whole only through Dionysus's rescue. Instead, according to Nietzsche, it is through her intense suffering that she overcomes heartbreak and overcomes herself. This triumph is reinforced by the fact that she chooses Dionysus. Nietzsche sees Dionysus as a heroic figure, but again, his interpretation is atypical. Nietzsche's Dionysus is not Ariadne's savior. Rather, he serves, in part, as the potential for Ariadne to recognize herself *in* and *for* herself.

## OVERCOMING SUFFERING BY EMBRACING IT

Heartbreak is both unquantifiable and complete. It's unquantifiable because it is a quality or state of being. It's complete because it permeates every part of one's being. De Chirico's Ariadne series gives us insight into how de Chirico grapples with heartbreak and provides us with some solace. The ways in which de Chirico's Ariadne differs from other versions of the myth and other artists' renditions offers us a view of his philosophical stance.

In Homer's account, for example, Ariadne is killed by Artemis shortly after she gives birth to Theseus's twin sons on Naxos. The murder was ordered by Dionysius because he was angry that Theseus and Ariadne had profaned his grotto with their love (or lovemaking, perhaps). In other versions, she kills herself after Theseus abandons her. In at least one version of the tale, Ariadne's sister, Phaedra, travels to Athens with Theseus and becomes his wife. In yet another account, Theseus abandons Ariadne only after Dionysus has told him that he, Dionysus, has decided to take her for his wife. In this account, a distraught Theseus forgets to change the sails on his boat from black to white—which was to be a signal to his father that he lived through the battle with the minotaur. When King Aegeus sees the sails of death, he flings himself into the sea. In the myth, all of these events were fated.

What do we make of this ongoing blood guilt? What does this tell us about the nature of heartbreak and suffering? When we look at the events surrounding the sleeping Ariadne, we see people swept up in events they do not design. We see people making choices only superficially, insofar as the ends are already fated. We see that, even when people make choices that are apparently independent of fate, these choices are based on limited knowledge. Let us suppose, for example, that Theseus had truly loved Ariadne, but that her beauty and devotion stirred the god, Dionysus, to claim her for his own. Whether she lived or died, she would endure overwhelming grief. In every version of this myth, Ariadne suffers a great deal. Suffering is transformative, for better and for worse. Through heartbreak, we are forever altered. It is perhaps for this reason that, unlike myriad depictions of Ariadne in the history of art where the young woman is an almost incidental figure, de Chirico chooses to dwell on her.

Although de Chirico's Ariadne series can be interpreted through a variety of lenses, including the development of his interaction with various art forms, our aim is to understand the series from de Chirico's standpoint regarding heartbreak and his Nietzschean philosophical themes. The series features the figure of Ariadne in the moments between sleep and wakefulness. Art historians disagree about how many paintings belong in the series—six, eight, or nine. But regardless of the exact number, there are sufficient parallels between at least eight of these paintings to help us begin weaving a coherent story of heartbreak. The selection and organization of the images in these paintings, combined with somber colors, the stark light of an utterly cloudless sky, and deep shadows indicative of autumn, are unsettling. They evoke a sense of foreboding and confusion.

Ordinary objects like clocks, trains, and smokestacks, commonplace locations like plazas and city squares, and architectural features like colonnades and turrets combine with the flat color palette and arrangement to give us the feeling of tense silence, isolation, and abandonment. Mysterious figures sporadically appear, typically shrouded in cloaks and facing away from us, or as tiny, indistinct figures. We can't tell whether they are walking toward us or away from us. We don't know whether they're talking or silent. Although each painting has different features, the one constant is Ariadne, who is solitary, both on the canvas and in her unknowing state of slumber.

Taken as a whole, the eight paintings tell the story of heartbreak and its transformation into an affirmation of life. Recurring elements in the series invite us to consider the ways in which Ariadne experiences the trauma of heartbreak and the catharsis of fully absorbing it. Assuming de Chirico follows the standard account of the Ariadne myth but infuses it with a Nietzschean interpretation of feminine power and Dionysian life-affirming creativity, the eight paintings depict Ariadne's impending heartache and her responses to it.

In each painting, she is depicted as a marble statue. De Chirico's Ariadne does nothing but sleep—or languish in that foggy moment between unconsciousness and consciousness. She does not act. She is alone in that singular moment. Rendered as stone, Ariadne is not the sensual representation of traditional paintings, not the eroticized figure upon which male painters impose their sexual objectification. This is perhaps our first indication that the Cretan princess is ultimately stronger than the fate about to befall her. If so, de Chirico expresses respect, rather than lust, for her. Although there is a long tradition of treating "Woman" as a lesser being or an appendage of man, in de Chirico's hands, she is complete in her own right. Perhaps also, the statue, as an immobile object, is indicative of the paralytic heartbreak, the sorrow, the isolation felt following a period of feeling embraced.

Another plausible interpretation of why de Chirico paints Ariadne as stone relates to the cult of Dionysus—paradoxical as this may seem. The stone Ariadne is inert, asexual, *infertile*. She is hardly a candidate for being a Dionysian woman. Yet the story goes that she chooses him and becomes his wife. This Ariadne is another sort of woman altogether. And why shouldn't she be? Given that the purportedly heroic Theseus betrayed the woman who made slaying the Minotaur possible, it should come as no surprise that on the rebound, she would turn her gaze toward the nonrational, lascivious, seemingly chaotic realm embodied by Dionysus.

The title of the first painting in the series, *Melanconia*, is a reference to the work of another artist (Albrecht Dürer) and to the Italian word for melancholy. In *Melanconia* the princess is facing us, and her pose is reminiscent of Nietzsche's "thinker" photograph and de Chirico's self-portrait that was styled after the Nietzsche pose. But rather than sitting upright like Nietzsche and de Chirico, Ariadne is reclining and resting on her left arm, looking lethargic. De Chirico portrays Ariadne in that suspended moment just before fully awakening to find herself abandoned by her lover. The barren calmness that permeates the scene is only momentary, for the viewer knows that beyond the canvas there will be chaos when Ariadne becomes aware of her solitary existence.

In (2) *The Melancholy of a Beautiful Day*, the sun is behind Ariadne, casting long shadows. She is positioned between a city in the background and a covered figure in the foreground. Here Ariadne is still the focus, but she is neither centered nor in the painting's foreground. She rests on a three-tiered base that doubles as a fountain and she is covering her eyes with her right arm. Perhaps she is crying over her fate.

The third painting in the series, (3) *The Red Tower*, features a tall round tower with small windows near the top that looks like a fortress. We see a statue of a horse with a rider, but only the front of the horse and just a portion of the rider are visible. We do not see Ariadne or anyone else in the painting. But if we look carefully at the lower left foreground, there are two shadows. One could be a reclining figure, while the other could be someone standing over it. In her exquisite suffering, Ariadne has lost herself completely.

In (4) *The Lassitude of the Infinite*, Ariadne's features are indistinct but her gaze is now directed upward. Perhaps she is slowly beginning to reemerge. Behind her, far in the background, two small figures appear in an otherwise deserted plaza, while a locomotive moves in the distance behind a low wall, illustrating the movement of time in one direction. Time moves as Ariadne remains still, perhaps representing the emotionally paralyzed wreckage of heartbreak. (We may even consider the train as a reference to de Chirico's own heartbreak. His father, a railroad engineer, died when de Chirico was a teenager.) The title may also be a reference to what de Chirico later described in his 1929 memoir as Nietzsche's "strange and profound poetry, infinitely and mysteriously solitary".[82] Lassitude, or weariness, or the infinite. The *unending*. Edges blur. All moments are now, and "now" is etched in pain.

In (5) *Ariadne*, the building's shadows reach toward the sleeping princess. In the distance, de Chirico presents the perspective of a locomotive's engine aligning with Ariadne's head, which is practically perpendicular to it. Meanwhile, fluttering turret flags suggest a breeze blowing in the opposite direction, and with it a ship in full (*white*) sail. Here Ariadne is again in the foreground, while both a train and a ship appear in the distance. Theseus has departed; Dionysus emerges.

(6) *The Soothsayer's Recompense* features Ariadne turned toward us, while long shadows from the building behind her darken the surroundings. Once again, we see a locomotive with a large white plume of smoke trailing behind it, but this time the train is heading to the painting's left edge. The train is behind a wall that separates Ariadne from events on the other side. Through a foreground arch, we see two palm trees tilting away from one another.

For what, we may wonder, and to whom is the soothsayer in the painting's title making amends? Who *is* the soothsayer? Perhaps the first question to ask is: *What* is a soothsayer? In Greek mythology, the soothsayer delivers prophesies. Most often, these are predictions of events that will be distressing to humans. Tiresias, perhaps the most famous of this class of soothsayers, foretold Oedipus's terrible future, in which he would kill his father and marry his mother.

But in de Chirico's hands, the soothsayer, or any foretelling of the future, is undone by time. This is the only painting in the series with a clock. While it has an hour hand and a minute hand, there are only 11 Roman numerals, suggesting that the end of the cycle is never reached. Does this mean that time is not linear, as we think of it as being? It may be, as Nietzsche proposed, that we shall live each and every moment of our lives as they are now, eternally. The breaking of Ariadne's heart, and all that goes with it, will occur again and yet again, forever.

(7) *Ariadne's Afternoon* is the only work in which the princess's face is turned toward the sun. Not entirely unlike the inhabitants of Plato's Cave, Ariadne opens her eyes and experiences *truth*. Bright sunlight is at first painful and makes her eyes blink, but it allows her to see reality – to emerge from the shadows of her pain.

(8) *The Joys and Enigmas of a Strange Hour* reflects Ariadne's embrace of her suffering. The acceptance of pain is bittersweet, possibly because we understand the relentless suffering of life on a subconscious level.

De Chirico's paintings are, in some sense, dreamscapes. The objects he paints don't have obvious meanings, and the puzzling pieces don't form a coherent picture. Each painting is fraught with the dissonance of colors, perspectives, light and shadows, emptiness, loneliness, and the strange anxiety generated in a dream. When we awaken, the content of the dream doesn't match the emotion that it generated. In each painting, nothing appears to be happening, and yet we feel the tension wrought by the awareness of suffering—whether it be our awareness of Ariadne's story, or our awareness of our own sorrow.

De Chirico's philosophical outlook combined with the surrealistic dreamscape forces us to question what we take to be real, true, and good. Even our concept of time as a linear process toward a specified end is upended by the eternity of the colonnades' geometric forms, the deserted squares, the shadows that grow long and then begin again. In these suspended moments, we are fully engaged in a form of existential crisis, both intellectually and emotionally.

## Transformation through Embracing Enigma

The Greek's equal embrace of joy and sorrow is something of an enigma. Most of us find it difficult to understand this willingness to gaze directly into the abyss. But de Chirico's Ariadne series suggests that the artist is comfortable with the enigma. For de Chirico and for Nietzsche, whose later work included critiques of all traditional metaphysics, including Classical Greek conceptions, reality is not knowable. It is fundamentally enigmatic. De Chirico said that man's desire to accept reality while simultaneously knowing that there is no such thing leads us to what he called "revelation."

To ponder the meaning of life—why we are here, why we were born, why we live, why we die—is peculiarly human, and also futile. De Chirico and Nietzsche maintain that there is no reason for any of it. "To live in the world as in a museum of strange things," de Chirico muses, "full of strange colourful toys that change their aspect and that sometimes, like children, we break to see what they are made of and disappointingly find that they are empty."[83] Our disappointing discovery of the emptiness of reality and the absence of truth leads us to despair or, more aptly, to melancholy. It is only in art, illusion, and myth that we can escape our misery, turning what is inherently intolerable into an object of beauty. The myth of Ariadne is an example of this view. Myth is always enigmatic.

De Chirico's pre-1915 paintings, specifically those in his Ariadne series, yearn for a return to an ideal, a yearning that he shares with Nietzsche, a self-proclaimed "student of more ancient times." De Chirico also appreciates the classical era, but knows very well that such a return is impossible. In her heartbreak, Ariadne yearns for reunion with her beloved, all the while knowing it is not to be. And so we enter melancholic reverie.

In Ariadne's heartbreak, she is utterly isolated, exiled from love, from the connections that had made her life meaningful. The series shows that she is wrought by anguish and eventually sinks into melancholy but is ultimately transformed. Melancholy, that pervasive feeling of sadness, is a stage through which we must pass as we gaze upon the enigma of life, which is revealed only fleetingly. In presenting Ariadne as he does, de Chirico straddles two worlds, the rational and the nonrational, the mortal and the immortal, Theseus's world and Dionysus's world. In sleep, Ariadne is about to be reborn.

While Ariadne sleeps, she is unaware of her fate. De Chirico forces us to *experience* enigma by way of the perspectival contrasts in each painting—we can't quite get hold of the center, as it were. Meaning is continually challenged. In de Chirico's series, the public squares are almost deserted. Every now and then a mysterious figure appears, but otherwise there are no people. Even Ariadne herself is captured in stone. The point, the purpose of the environment, is left unrealized.

This all makes more sense when we view de Chirico's art through his fascination with Nietzsche and his philosophy. De Chirico said, "It is only with Nietzsche that I can say I have begun a real life."[84] This statement naturally raises the question: We eat, sleep, breathe, work, study—isn't that living? Yes and no. From de Chirico's point of view, our actions are no more than expressions of brute existence, unless they are *purposefully* directed in specific ways. This line of thinking suggests that our orientation toward life is what determines how we survive heartbreak and how it transforms us. De Chirico demonstrates that we will be in a much better position to transform ourselves and overcome heartbreak if we fully embrace the concept that life, in and of itself, is pointless. His interpretation of the Ariadne myth shows that by embracing enigma we are liberated and can create our own meaning.

What we call myth, others call reality. Whatever else it might do, myth typically attempts to explain events in terms of gods. For example, myth tells us that earthquakes are caused by Poseidon, the god of water, horses, and earthquakes. The mythological gods were the embodiment of natural causes and events that could not be explained. But myths are not simply stories that we tell ourselves when we can't make sense of what's happening. Myths are social stabilizers. Through structured stories, myths instruct us on how to live. They remind us of what's most important to us. It is from these stories that, according to Nietzsche, tragedy emerges as a means of coping with "the value of existence." The myths of the Greek gods Apollo, Dionysus, and Heraclitus were most influential for de Chirico and Nietzsche. As mythical figures, Apollo and Dionysus represent light, clarity, measure, and the harmony of reason, on the one hand, and darkness, frenzy, excess, and the chaos of emotional irrationality, on the other. Heraclitus emphasizes the tensions and ultimate unity between opposites. Perhaps most famous for the saying, "You cannot step into the same river twice," Heraclitus saw harmony between these opposites.

As Aristotle explained it, the standard Greek tragedy represents a hero or heroine moving through the stages of an action that has serious implications, is complete, and has magnitude.[85] The action is typically related to the hero or heroine's deep desire to achieve some goal or other—for Oedipus, it was to avoid the soothsayer Tieresis's terrible prophesy, for Antigone, to bury her brother. The hero's goal, no matter how noble it may be, often reflects some flaw, hubris, or ego that is utterly impotent in the face of fate or the gods' wills. It also reflects limitations in the individual or society. According to Aristotle, these limitations result in a reversal in fortune, but also in transformation. Though the hero or heroine misses the mark, he or she learns something, and in this process, there is "a change from ignorance to awareness of a bond of love or hate."[86] For us, there is *catharsis*, typically a purging of feelings of pity or fear for the hero or heroine. In this way, we live vicariously through the characters and feel genuine emotion without enduring the actual events that are depicted.

Both myth and tragedy reflect a Greek view of life that is far from synonymous with gentility, harmony, and the primacy of rationality. This is what Nietzsche thinks is crucial for understanding the real value of Classical Greece. Dionysus is associated with the birth of tragedy and Aristotle created a formal theory of tragedy, but theorizing about tragedy is not the same as creating or living it.

"There is an ancient story," Nietzsche tells us, "that King Midas hunted in the forest a long time for the wise Silenus, the companion of Dionysus."[87] When Silenus was finally captured, being wise, he initially refused to answer the king's question, "What is the best and most desirable of all things for man?" Eventually, however, Silenus exclaimed, "What is best of all is beyond your reach forever: not to be born, not to *be,* to be *nothing.* But the second best for you—is quickly to die." Nietzsche asserts that this reveals "the terror and horror of existence," but more importantly, it reflects the Greek capacity to "again and again overcome."

From Nietzsche's perspective, the real value of Greek tragedy is that it teaches us how to live in the inexorable face of horror. The Greeks did not run from it or even look away. They rejoiced. They taught us that to live is to embrace, and in so doing, to overcome existence. There is no resolution, per se, only a decision to passionately embrace life as it is, whereby we are redeemed.

# HEARTBREAK CAN INSPIRE CREATIVITY

Nietzsche's deep affinity for the Greeks may have been inspired by Dionysian suffering, in which what Dionysius endured in utero and as an infant was transfigured into a life-affirming reality. Despite the terrible suffering that occurs in their ancient stories, despite the fact that Dionysus gave birth to tragedy, the Greeks embraced their lives exactly as they were. Most of us, upon hearing that Odysseus must leave his beloved Penelope to go on a long voyage the very day their son is born, are angry or at least dismayed or disappointed. When Odysseus doesn't return and his castle is taken over by suitors demanding a chance to win Penelope's hand—and the kingdom—we shake our fists at the gods. "You have no *right*!" we say, with righteous indignation. But Penelope doesn't cry or rage. Instead, she tells the suitors that she will select one of them when she finishes weaving a burial shroud for Odysseus's elderly father. And each night she quietly unravels the weaving on her loom, buying herself another day. Despite the horrors of existence—brutal wars, the apparently ruthless vicissitudes of the gods' and humans' almost utter inability to *do* anything about it—despite all this, the ancient Greeks celebrated life. What else is Dionysus but the embodiment of such glorification?

And what about Ariadne? She who had given Theseus the string by which he escaped the labyrinth? She who had given *herself* upon Theseus's promise and betrayed her half-brother, her father and her city? She to whom Dionysus reputedly proclaimed, "I am your labyrinth"? What makes her worthy of our deepest sympathy? What makes her so worthy of Nietzsche's admiration that he referred to his lover as his Ariadne and himself as Dionysus? What has she embraced?

To answer those questions, we need to take a look at several interrelated concepts that are central to Nietzsche's thoughts about suffering, eternal recurrence, and overcoming difficulty, thoughts that may have intensified as he descended into madness in his forties. First, for Nietzsche, Greek culture was exemplified by two principles: the Apollonian (rational, analytical) and the Dionysian (ecstatic, emotional). Ariadne embodies both of these principles. For all she knows, she has been abandoned. Reason does not provide answers to all of life's questions. In her misery, in her abject loneliness and suffering, she is primed to be absorbed into the Dionysian. She sleeps between Dionysus and his half-brother Apollo, to whom the sacrifices in the Minotaur's labyrinth were made. As we know, there is no definitive reason for Ariadne's suffering. It is without meaning. It is not something we can understand. We want reasons, which are typically equated with meaning. We understand Event B in light of Event A, which explains it. Not so with Ariadne. Not so with heartbreak. Not so with *life*. She suffers, but *for what*?

For Nietzsche, life is inherently without meaning. We can view the universe as purposeful—objects and life forms make sense where and how they exist. We can also view the universe as mechanical—it's not imbued with meaning, but it's not meaningless either. In other words, to the extent that meaning can be *made*, for example, through techno-logical advances, it can be improved or worked on. With *that*, then, come concepts like guilt and blame, responsibil-ity and punishment.

When we consider suffering in light of these possibilities, there appears to be nothing worse than meaningless suffer-ing. In the standard telling of the myth, we never know why Theseus abandons Ariadne. She suffers for no discernible rea-son. Her suffering is meaningless. It is what it is, rather than what we think it should be. Like any inexplicable horror, we believe it should be otherwise. But this view only makes sense if we believe that the universe is either inherently meaningful or at least malleable. If the universe is as Nietzsche has it, the horror can never be explained.

If we cannot change senseless suffering, what makes us think we can change anything? Is this perception what prompted Nietzsche to allegedly wrap his arms around a coach horse who was being abused and then suffer a mental breakdown? Perhaps in our suffering, we wish there were an-other world in place of this one, or at the very least, that we were not in it as we are. But is this really what we want?

Ariadne lies as stone. Inert. Her fate has been cast by the long line of circumstances that began with a magical string. Should she not rage against it? Should she not rant and scream for something different—anything but *this*? But what good would that do? How could she will the *past* to be different, when her will is always directed forward? Why doesn't she collapse from the weight of the pain devouring her? Should she simply end it all? Wouldn't that eliminate what is otherwise impossible to discard?

Wait. The truth is that we can be swallowed up by heartbreak or we can find a way to embrace our life in every aspect, *as if we will live it again and again.* We can choose to peer into the abyss, affirm it, and *not* be swallowed up by it. This is where our power emerges, where we transform from something that has *happened to us* to what we *will for ourselves.* In our terrible suffering, we say, "Yes. I accept, I *embrace*, I *want* this suffering." Do we wallow? No! Do we fight? No! Do we beg and plead with our lover to return, crawling on knees scabbed over by a lifetime of fear? No! No! No! We do none of these things. Because none of these things is equivalent to embracing our suffering *as ours.* We can love this moment as much as any other we have lived or will live. We have no reason to wish it were different, because in a meaningless universe, events occur without our agreement or approval. And when friends and family come to give us solace, to *pity* us, we turn them away. We are offended by their attempt to impose their meaning on us. Whether the universe is meaningless or not doesn't really matter. What matters is our disposition toward life. What matters is how we use the energy of our heartbreak and suffering to create meaning and to express our deepest truths with creativity.

When we *will* our life to be as it is, when we love our life enough to say that we would live it exactly as it is forever, we overcome the stranglehold of heartbreak and suffering.

When we acknowledge that heartbreak is an opportunity for us to transform, create, and rejoice, we can accept that our hearts may be broken again and again. While the concept of a meaningless universe may seem dire, when we consider it more closely we see that it is both liberating and inspiring. In a universe without meaning, we create the meaning ourselves. We can choose to be victors instead of victims. We can choose to embrace heartbreak and allow it to enrich our lives. We can transform the energy of sorrow and despair into mesmerizing art, music, and poetry. We can. And we will. *Amor fati.*

1. George Santayana, "Normal Madness," *Dialogues in Limbo, with Three New Dialogues* (Ann Arbor: U of Michigan, 1957), 41.

2. Pablo Neruda and W. S. Merwin, *Twenty Love Poems and a Song of Despair* (London: Jonathan Cape, 1969).

3. Pedro Salinas, *My Voice Because of You*, Trans. Willis Barnstone (Albany: State University of New York Press, 1977).

4. George Gordon Byron and Holger Drachmann, *Don Juan* (Kjøbenhavn: Schubothes Boghandels Forlag, 1880), 119.

5. Quoted in Roth Katz Crispin, "'¡Qué verdad revelada!' The poet and the absent beloved of Pedro Salinas's *La voz a ti debida, Razon de amor,* and *Largo Lamento*," *Revista Hispánica Moderna* 54 (2001): 111.

6. Francesco Petrarca, Gianfranco Contini, and Daniele Ponchiroli, Il *Canzoniere* (Torino: G. Einaudi, 1964). The translation is from Francesco Petrarca and David Young, *The Poetry of Petrarch* (New York: Farrar, Straus and Giroux, 2004).

7.  Dominic Moran, *Pablo Neruda* (London: Reaktion, 2009), 20.

8.  Quoted in Semir Zeki, *Splendors and Miseries of the Brain: Love, Creativity and the Quest for Human Happiness* (Chichester: Wiley-Blackwell, 2008), 105.

9.  Jason Wilson, *A Companion to Pablo Neruda: Evaluating Neruda's Poetry* (Woodbridge: Tamesis, 2008), 47.

11. Early critics of *La voz a ti debida*, despite its title suggesting it was addressed to a woman of flesh and blood, held that the collection was not in the least autobiographical and went so far as to say that it did not even concern itself with love. According to Leo Spitzer, the poem is "the lament of a soul who, lacking faith in God, seeks fulfilment in self-knowledge." ("El conceptismo interior de Pedro Salinas", Revista Hispánica Moderna, VII, 1941, 37). Others such as Darmangeat insist the "tú" Salinas directs his words towards is an imaginary being that is merely the symbolic incarnation of the general concept of love and for Díaz-Plaja, the beloved from the collection was little more than a projection of a Neoplatonic ideal.

    We now know that this is far from the case. In July 1999, the Salinas archive held by Harvard University Library was opened to reveal more than 355 letters from Pedro Salinas to Katherine Reding confirming she had been his lover and muse, despite him having a wife and family throughout the affair. The archive also held a memoir written by Reding. aptly titled "La amada de Pedro Salinas", thus removing any doubts about her existence. Her reply to the critics who questioned her presence in the poetry was rather understanding of their claims: "sonreí cuando leí sus [critics Leo Spitzer and Ángel del Río] resañas, pero creo que tenían razón en parte."

Salinas met Reding in Madrid in the summer of 1932, when Reding, a visiting graduate student from Smith College in America, took a class Salinas taught on the Generation of 1898. She writes of their first encounter: "that was it: *un flechazo*; lighting had struck; the pursuit had begun." Salinas confirms it was love at first sight in the twelfth poem of *La voz a ti debida* where he writes, "yo no necesito tiempo para saber cómo eres: conocerse es el relámpago." The ambiguity that led critics to doubt the existence of an actual beloved can be understood biographically, for the nature of the Salinas-Reding relationship was clandestine, given that Salinas was married with children. Nonetheless Salinas, was, unsurprisingly, elated over the reaction to his book and speculation about his muse that arose in 1933 and wrote to Reding shortly after its publication, where he referred to himself as "Don juan-Salinas". Beyond the questionable humour of this statement, the same letter reveals, in perhaps a more serious tone, his sentiments:

"Ay, mi Katherine, la verdad es que todo el mundo sin conocerte te siente… [Pero] los demás, hasta los que mas cerca viven, solo me conocen en partes mayores o menores. Tú, lejana y próxima, eres, Katherine, la única que sabe quien es Pedro y lo que quiere ser…"

It is possible that it is because she is "lejana y próxima" that he can love her as passionately as he claims to in his letters. It is also expressed in *El Chantajista*, in which Salina's protagonist, Lisardo perfectly expresses the benefit of loving a woman through letters: "Es tan romantico amarse por carta. Se dicen tantas cosas que los labios no dirían  Las mujeres son, para eso de las cartas, únicas."

Perhaps understanding this, Reding displayed some prudence in accepting the grand statements in Salinas' letters. She scribbled on the back of an envelope of another letter he had written her in 1935: "beautiful letter in which he assures me that he loves me *as I am* – which, poor dear, he could never quite do except when my actions coincided with his ideas." We will see this to be the case in both Salinas and Neruda.

Reding stresses in her foreword to the Houghton Library archives: "mi querido Pedro, con su amor y nostalgia inventó verdaderamente su infinito." I do not doubt for a minute that it is because Reding was "lejana y próxima" that she could remain everything that Salinas desired and envisioned. Reality is always far more mundane than poetry; Salinas evades this by creating his ideal woman, who albeit shares characteristics with his real-life beloved, is recreated in his mind's eye. This is paralleled in Neruda's poem, 'El prisionero', which was replaced in 1932 with Poem 9. 'El prisionero' echoes the importance of the beloved's absence for poetic creation, as it impels the poet to feel deeply:

Líbrame de tu amor mujer lejana y bella
Que por bella y lejana me dueles cada día

Returning to Salinas, C.B. Morris wrote in *A Generation of Spanish Poets* that "… to possess his *amada* would thwart Salinas' ambition to live perpetually cocooned within a love from which he excluded the banal data of time, place, and circumstances…. Salinas was more interested in probing and weighing (love's) effects on his sensibility than in imagining what it could look like."[11]

"Although Reding says that any reader of the book has access to a description of this early phase of the affair, implying that it is reasonably accurate, she also says that its *tú* is far from being recognizably she, so that in a way, as she points out, Leo Spitzer and Ángel del Río had not been entirely wrong to think that the book was not about a real woman. And she adds that she has no sense of Salinas' need to be Pygmalion to her Galatea (the comparison is hers), as "Allí detrás de la risa" (11) and "Perdóname por ir así buscándote" (41), among other strophes in the poem, imply. In fact she was a woman with a profession and career, during a period when such a life was hardly common; it thus unlikely that she was the frivolous or capricious young woman portrayed in many parts of *La voz*, in need of a more adult male to inspire and guide her re-invention as a mature, sober and serious person."

12. Whitmore, Katherine Prue (Reding). *La amada de Pedro Salinas* (Pasadena: University of California Press, 1979), 381.

13. In *Jorge Manrique: O, Tradición Y Originalidad* (Buenos Aires: Editorial Sudamericana, 1962), Pedro Salinas writes that in the tradition of courtly love, marriage is dulled by duty and bondage, whereas the extramarital affair implies freedom. Salinas's analysis of Manrique certainly provides insight into his own sentiments.

14. Jorge Edwards, *La otra casa: Ensayos sobre escritores Chilenos* (Santiago: Ediciones Universidad Diego Portales, 2006), 82. Translation my own

15. Pablo Neruda, *Confieso que he vivido: Memorias* (Barcelona: Editorial Seix Barral, 1974), 75–76.

16. Emir Rodríguez Monegal, *El viajero inmóvil* (Buenos Aires: Losada, 1966), 49.

17. Neruda wrote in *Reflexiones sobre Isla Negra 65* (OC V, p. 233): "Me sorprendieron los ojos negros de María Parodi. Más tarde escribí para ella el número diecinueve de mis *Veinte poemas*" ("I was moved by Maria Parodi's flashing dark eyes. Later, it was for her that I wrote Poem 19 of *Twenty Poems*")

18. Katherine Prue Whitmore (Reding), *La amada de Pedro Salinas* (Houghton Library, Harvard University, 1999), 5.

19. Pedro Salinas, *La poesía de Rubén Darío* (Barcelona: Seix Barral, 1975), 10.

20. Pedro Salinas, *La Poesia,* 10.

21. The "traje verde" described by Salinas seems to be directly borrowed from Petrarch's Sonnet 12, where Laura's green clothes make the lover weep ("i Verdi panni, / e 'l viso scolorir che ne' miei danni / a llamentar mi fa pauroso et lento").

22. These desires are Platonic in nature. See the allegory of the cave in Book VII of Plato, *Republic*, trans. G.M.A. Grube (Indianapolis: Hackett, 1974).

23. J.M. Aguirre, "La voz a ti debida: Salinas y Bergson, *Revue de Littérature Comparée* 52 (1978): 98–118.

25. Cortázar, Julio. *Obra Crítica*. Ed. Saúl Sosnowski. Vol. 3. Madrid: Alfagura, 1994. P. 66

English translation appears in Cortázar, Julio. *Obra Crítica*. Ed. Saúl Sosnowski. Vol. 3. Madrid: Alfagura, 1994. P. 30

25. For a further analysis of the sexual depiction of the beloved in Neruda's *Veinte poemas de amor*, see Dominic Moran, "Cuerpo de mujer: Neruda's Sex Education," *Hispanic Research Journal* (London), 10 (2009): 56–69.

26. Francesco Petrarca and J.G. Nichols, "200," *Canzoniere* (New York: Routledge, 2002)

27. Francesco Petrarca and J.G. Nichols, "306," *Canzoniere* (New York: Routledge, 2002). N. pag.

28. In Poem 10, the lovers are described in the plural—"hemos perdido aun este crepúsculo" ("we have lost even this twilight")—yet this is undermined because they aren't currently together.

29. Carlos Feal Deibe, *La poesía de Pedro Salinas* (Madrid: Editorial Gredos, 1965), 75–76.

30. Miguel de Unamuno, *Obras Completas*, Vol. 2 (Madrid: A. Aguado, 1958), 837.

31. Carlos Feal Deibe, *La poesía de Pedro Salinas* (City: Publisher, Year), 75–76. Author's translation.

32. The motif can be seen in Petrarch's Sonnet 249: "*tra belle, donne, a guisa d'una rosa tra minor' fior*" ("among fair ladies, like a rose among the lesser flowers").

33. In the *Symposium*, Diotima describes love as a ladder that leads from the lower form (love for a specific individual) to a higher form (love of the good and the beautiful).

34. Arthur Schopenhauer, "World as Will and Idea," in *The Philosophy of Erotic Love*, ed. Robert C. Solomon and Kathleen Marie Higgins (Lawrence: University Press of Kansas, 1991), 121.

35. Julian Palley, "La Voz a Ti Debida: An Appreciation," *Hispania* 40.4 (1957): 450.

36. Miguel de Unamuno, *Del sentimiento tragico de la vida* (Marid: Akal editor, 1983), 286. Author's translation.

37. Jason Wilson, *A Companion to Pablo Neruda: Evaluating Neruda's Poetry* (Woodbridge: Tamesis, 2008), 50.

38. Gustavo Adolfo Bécquer, "Rima LXIV," in *Rimas y Leyendas* (Barcelona: Linkgua, 2007), 51.

39. .

40. Percy Bysshe Shelley and Mary Wollstonecraft Shelley, *A Defence of Poetry* (Indianapolis: Bobbs-Merrill, 1904), 71.

41. Unamuno, *Del sentimiento tragico*, 286.

42. R. Martínez Nadal, "Guía al lector de *El público*," in Federico García Lorca, *El público y Comedia sin título: Dos obras teatrales postumas*(Barcelona: Seix Barral, 1979), 236. Author's translation.

43. The Residencia de Estudiantes itself was a hotbed of intellectual, political, scientific, and artistic activity. Founded in 1910, it was already considered Spain's major cultural institution by the time Dalí arrived 12 years later. Intended to complement the formal university education of its charges, the Resi cultivated fertile ground by promoting *conversaciones* through hosting conferences, literary lectures, and concerts, welcoming avant-garde artists and scientists, and generally fostering the creative environment in which the likes of John Meynard Keyes, José Ortega y Gasset, Miguel de Unamuno, Albert Einstein, Igor Stravinsky, and Marie Curie could talk, listen, explore, experiment, and discover. The ideas generated in this environment extended beyond Spanish culture to also influence the broader European culture.

44. John Baxter, *Buñuel* (London: Fourth Estate, 1994), 160.

45. Salvador Dalí, *Ma vie secrete* (Paris: Editions de La Table Ronde, 1952),

46. Dalí, *Ma vie secrete,* page.

47. Dalí, *Ma vie secrete,* page.

48. Mary Ann Caws, *Salvador Dalí* (London: Reaktion, 2008).

49. Interestingly, Lorca had a marked-up copy of Oscar Wilde's *De Profundis* and knew about his imprisonment in England.

50. Fèlix Fanés, "Surrealism's Moral Stance," *Salvador Dalí: The Construction of the Image, 1925–1930* (New Haven: Yale University Press, 2007), 175.

51. Gema Pérez-Sánchez, "Spanish Literature in the Long Twentieth Century, 1898–2007," in *The Cambridge History of Gay and Lesbian Literature*, ed E. L. McCallum and Mikko Tuhkanen (City: Publisher, Year), 640-42.

52. Federico García Lorca, Gwynne Edwards, and Peter Luke, *Plays: One (Lorca, Federico Garcia)* (London: Methuen, Year): 14.

53. Speaking of his parents in a letter to the playwright Eduardo Marquina, Lorca wrote: "They are displeased with me and do nothing but point to the example of my brother Paquito, a student at Oxford loaded with laurels." José Montero Alonso, *Vida De Eduardo Marquina* (Madrid: Editora Nacional, 1965), 205.

54. Federico García Lorca and Miguel García-Posada, *Obras Completas*, vol. III (Barcelona: Círculo De Lectores, 1997), 910-11. Author's translation.

55. Gypsy Ballads of 1924-1927

56. Salvadore Dalí, *The Secret Life of Salvador Dalí* (New York: Dover, 1993), 203.

57. Leslie Stainton, *Lorca: A Dream of Life* (New York: Farrar, Straus, Giroux, 1999), 132.

58. For their letters, see Victor Fernández, Rafael Santos Torroella, Salvador Dalí, and Federico García Lorca, *Querido Salvador, Querido Lorquito: Epistolario 1925–1936* (City: Publisher, Year).

59. Federico García Lorca and Christopher Maurer, *Deep Song and Other Prose* (New York: New Directions, 1980), 87.

60. Rafael Martínez Nadal and Federico García Lorca, *Federico García Lorca: Mi Penúltimo Libro Sobre El*

*Hombre Y El Poeta; Con 30 Cartas Inéditas, 23 De Lorca, 15 Dibujos También Inéditos, 6 De Lorca, 9 De José Caballero, Y 11 Fotografías Igualmente Inéditas.* (Madrid: Casariego, 1992), 56.

61. Salvador Dalí, letter published in *El Pais*, Madrid, 30 January 1986.

62. Born Elena Ivanovna Diakonova.

63. Lorca and García-Posada, *Obras Completas*, Vol. VI, 979.

64. Lorca and García-Posada, *Obras Completas*, Vol.III, 1011.

65. Lorca and García-Posada, *Obras Completas*, Vol. III, 1020.

66. Lorca and García-Posada, *Obras Completas*, Vol. VI, 1024.

67. Lorca and García-Posada, *Obras Completas*, Vol. VI, 1079.

68. Federico García Lorca, Christopher Maurer, and Andrew A. Anderson, *Epistolario Completo* (Madrid: Cátedra, 1997), 574–75.

69. Javier Pérez Andújar, *Salvador Dalí: A La Conquista De Lo Irracional* (Madrid: Algaba Ediciones, 2003), 145.

70. Salvador Dalí, *The Secret Life of Salvador Dalí*, page.

71. Ian Gibson, *The Shameful Life of Salvador Dalí* (New York: W.W. Norton, 1998), 107–108.

72. Derek Harris, *Federico García Lorca: Poeta En Nueva York* (London: Grant and Cutler, 1978), 9.

73. Federico García Lorca and David Gershator. *Selected Letters* (New York: New Directions, 1983), 146.

74. Lorca, and Gershator. *Selected Letters*, 148.

75. Georges Bataille, *Literature and Evil*, trans. Alastair Hamilton (London: Marion Boyars, 1990), 48.

76. Søren Kierkegaard, Bruce H. Kirmmse, and Niels Jørgen. Cappelørn. What is this? "Journal AA: 12 - 1835." *Kierkegaard's Journals and Notebooks* (Princeton: Princeton UP, 2007), 21–22.

77. For more on this, see Søren Kierkegaard, Howard V. Hong, and Edna H. Hong, *Works of Love: Some Christian Reflections in the Form of Discourses* (New York: Harper, 1962).

78. Lorca and García-Posada, *Obras Completas*. Vol. VI, 979.
    Coney Island es una gran feria a la cual los domingos de verano acuden más de un millón de criaturas.

Beben, gritan, comen, se revuelan y dejan del mar llenos de periódicos y las calles abarrotadas de latas, de cigarros apagados, de mordiscos, de zapatos sin tacón. Vuelve la muchedumbre de la feria cantando y vomita en grupos de cien personas apoyadas sobre las barandillas de los embarcaderos, y orina en grupos de mil en los rincones, sobre los barcos abandonados y sobre los monumentos de Garibaldi o el soldado desconocido

79. García Lorca, *Obras completas,* Is this the same anthology as in the previous note? vol. 3, pp. 163–73. What is the page on which the quotation appears? The translation is by Gwynne Edwards. Is the translation part of this volume?

80. R. Wicks, "Friedrich Nietzsche," *The Stanford Encyclopedia of Philosophy*, ed. Edward N. Zalta (Summer 2011).

81. Giorgio de Chirico, *Noi metafisici*, published in «Cronache d'attualità» Rome, 15 February 1919.

82. Giorgio de Chirico, *The Memoirs of Giorgio De Chirico* (New York: Da Capo, 1994), 55. *'the strange and profound poetry, infinitely mysterious and solitary, which is based on the Stimmung (I use this this very effective German word which could be translated as atmosphere in the moral sense), the Stimmung, I repeat, of an autumn afternoon, when the sky is clear and the shadows are longer than in summer, for*

*the sun is beginning to lower' (The Memoirs of Giorgio de Chirico, London, 1971, p. 55).*

83. Giorgio de Chirico, *Hebdomeros* (Paris: Éditions Du Carrefour, 1929), 186.

84. Giorgio de Chirico, Letter to Fritz Gartz, undated (January 5, 1911 reprinted and translated in Paolo Picozza,"Giorgio de Chirico and the Birth of Metaphysical Art in Florence in 1910," *Metafsica: Queaderni della Fondaziones Giorgio e Isa de Chirico no. 7/8* (2007–2008): 66.

85. Aristotle and Gerald Frank Else, *Poetics* (Ann Arbor: University of Michigan(1970), 25.

86. Esa Roos, *Medea: Myth and Unconscious Fantasy* 44.

87. Friedrich Wilhelm Nietzsche, Francis Golffing, and Friedrich Wilhelm Nietzsche, *The Birth of Tragedy; And, the Genealogy of Morals* (8)